T.E.A.R.S.

OF

JOY

THE PROCESS FOR PERSONAL TRANSFORMATION

ANDREW JOBLING

Ark House Press
arkhousepress.com

Cataloguing in Publication Data:
Title: T.E.A.R.S. Of Joy
ISBN: 978-0-6452569-4-9 (pbk)
Subjects: Christian Living;
Other Authors/Contributors: Jobling, Andrew

Design by initiateagency.com

CONTENTS

FOREWORD

It's not easy being a human being; it's an immense privilege, but it's not easy. There are so many challenges, so many choices, so many voices, so many pathways. They all lead to very different destinations. It was said in ancient times, *All roads lead to Rome*. It isn't true. Some roads lead to Death Valley, and Death Valley just isn't Rome. If you would prefer to end up in Rome rather than Death Valley, get hold of a reliable map, or at least ask someone who knows the way.

Just two years ago, in 2019, I found myself in need of a reliable map. I was one of three speakers at a one-day men's conference, which is where I first met Andrew Jobling – the author of the book you are holding in your hands. I did my two sessions and then sat back to listen. The next speaker, Dr Adrian Turner, did his doctorate in human transformation, so I was suitably impressed and listened with interest. His message focused on the latest research around the universal reality of phases in life, each phase usually lasting between seven to ten years. There is always a period of transition between these phases, a season of life that can be confusing, troubling, and even disturbing, yet a season that must be negotiated well to engage successfully with the next phase of life. As he spoke, I realised I was in one of those transitions. According to his time scale, my transition was leading into the final phase of my effective working life. I was 71 years old at that time and had been asking myself all the questions he described as indicative of a transition. It got my attention. He warned of the danger of getting stuck in a transition, and I realised I was at risk of doing just that. It was that realisation that set me up for the next speaker, Andrew Jobling.

Andrew talked to us about the message from his seventh book, *The Wellness Puzzle*. Andrew challenged the idea that our health and wellness can be viewed as one of the pillars in our life, along with other pillars like finance, relationships, and advancement in our profession. He stated that health is not a pillar – it is the foundation on which everything else is built. Lose your health, and nothing works. If I were to transition well into the final phase of my effective working life, my health and wellness had to be seen as the foundation of the future. I went home that day with the determination that things had to change.

I weighed 121.5 kg at that time. I never made a deliberate decision to make Death Valley my destination, but that was the road I was travelling. I tried for two weeks to make the changes alone. I quickly realised I needed help. I needed a guide, I needed a map, and I needed a coach. So, I phoned Andrew, he put on his Batman suit and answered the call. That decision has changed my life.

Since that time, I've dropped more than 20 kg and developed some vital skills I will carry with me for the rest of my life. In addition, I'm on the road to Rome, Paris, London, New York, and many other amazing places.

Now, let's talk about the book you are holding in your hands, 'TEARS of joy.' I had the privilege of being one of the first to read the manuscript. In fact, I took it away with me on holiday in preparation for writing the foreword you are reading. I appreciate the help Andrew has given me, so I was glad to have the opportunity to honour his kindness and gracious friendship by writing it. Of course, being asked to write a foreword is an honour in itself. However, what I didn't expect was another dramatic encounter. In reading this book, I was alerted to issues in my life that impacted me as much as my encounter with *The Wellness Puzzle*. I'm a little bit shocked by the significance of its message, actually.

Andrew's humility, insights and openhearted honesty allowed me to identify an opportunity to change my thinking that sorely needed to be addressed. I realised an attitude had developed in my thinking and that my emotions were sabotaging my hopes and dreams. This disappointment had coalesced into a roadblock. It can happen to any of us in our life's journey as we negotiate the *slings and arrows of outrageous fortune*. Thankfully, this book not only helped identify the problem it also helped in framing a solution. There are tools for life in this book, and I am employing them in addressing that roadblock. I shall not remain the same.

This book is a pathway to better days. It is a roadmap to greater joy, and for many, I have no doubt that its title will prove to be your experience, 'TEARS of joy'. But, if you do more than read it, if you follow the path Andrew has walked and employ the tools he has provided toward the end of this book, you will not be disappointed. I have printed out those tools and they are on the wall in front of my desk as I write the words you are reading.

So, take this book and do what I did. I read it, but then I did more than read it. I heard its message and allowed it to grip my attention to the point of action. I'm doing the stuff. Who knows, maybe we will bump into each other in Rome someday, or Paris, or London or maybe even Heaven itself. If this book does for you what it did for me, I'll see you there.

Dr Allan R Meyer
Author, Speaker, Leader
Co-founder of Careforce Lifekeys International
www.careforcelifekeys.org

INTRODUCTION

In 1970, a young man in his early twenties was driving home after working a long night shift. He was driving on a quiet country road at 6:00 am on a cold and icy Sunday in winter. He was listening to some heavy rock music on his eight-track tape player to keep himself awake after a busy night. As commonly happened with audiotape players in the '70s (if you're old enough to recall), tapes often got tangled in the machine. Well, it happened to this young man, and just as the tape stopped playing, the stereo automatically switched over to the radio. Somehow, in the middle of nowhere, the radio reception kicked in, and the moment the radio came on, a song finished, and the DJ said: "That was 'Joy to the World' by *Three Dog Night*". He went on to say: "If you're driving now, be careful of the slippery roads. In fact, put on your seatbelt. It may just save your life".

Seatbelts in the 1970s were more of a decorative addition to a car than anything used as a life preservation device. However, the DJ's words triggered a message from God and a thought in that young man's mind. He reached over, grabbed the seat belt, slung it across his chest and buckled it up. Less than one minute later, a truck coming in the other direction veered onto the wrong side of the road and was heading straight at him. The young man braked, swerved, slid, and skidded over the edge of the embankment. The car rolled end over end as several eight-track tapes hit the young man in the head. He thought he was going to die. Finally, the car came to rest upside down.

The young man was shaken, a little bruised, but okay, and was hanging upside down by his seatbelt. The engine had come through the firewall and was sitting right next to his face making a loud hissing sound. He was shaking, took a deep breath and thought, *in the movies, the next thing that happens is… BOOM!*

He somehow got free from the tangled mess, crawled out through the smashed window, and climbed up the embankment to the road where he was able to flag down a passing car. In less than thirty minutes, the ambulance and police were on the scene. The ambulance officer treated the young man for minor abrasions and shock. The police officer went to look at the wreck before climbing back up the embankment. He went over to the young man and handed him a section of the seatbelt he had cut out of the car. He said: "Keep this as a memento and show it to your children and grandchildren". He also said: "Son, I don't know why you were wearing a seatbelt, but it saved your life. I've been at wreck scenes like this for over twenty years, and let me tell you, that's a fatality!"

I was listening to this man telling this story about his car crash on an audio fifty years after it had happened, and he is no longer a young man. He now has four children and ten grandchildren. He has developed incredible success and wealth for himself and his family. He has positively impacted an untold number of lives, and created a legacy that will live on for generations to come. But how easily it could have all been different.

If it were not for a simple, seemingly insignificant thought – a message from God he paid attention to – he could have died on that winter morning in 1970. His response to that message was to put on his seat belt, and it was followed by a wonderful domino effect.

My question to you is this. If you knew and believed that everything you have and will have in your life, good or bad, happy or sad, healthy or unhealthy, starts with a thought, belief or perspective you choose to focus on, would you pay more attention to your thoughts?

I know that's a direct, strong, and confronting question to ask in the opening of a book, but I'm not here to waste your precious time. I've written this book to help you live a life of joyful longevity. That means a long life full of purpose, passion, prosperity, fun, fulfilment, love, joy, and laughter. How does that sound to you? While some people live a long life, they are unhappy, and there are far too many people whose lives are cut short. I'm not sure if you realise it or believe it, but we hold the power to determine the incredible life we live – not in our hands – in our head.

Many people believe their destiny, luck, success, and time on the planet is predetermined, and is mostly outside of their control. Well, I would like to challenge that a little. While it is true there are certain things outside of our control, we do get to control the most important thing that will direct and determine the type of life we live. That thing is our thoughts – every thought counts. Every thought will start a domino effect that will ripple out and impact your life and the lives of people around you. Every thought will be the foundational starting point for you to live a purposeful life of joyful longevity.

I'm sure most people have watched the *Rocky* movies or at least the first one. If you haven't, I recommend them all to you wholeheartedly. The last scene of the first *Rocky* movie sees Rocky, after fifteen brutal rounds with the world heavyweight champion Apollo Creed, with his face beaten and bloodied. Rocky is yelling for his girlfriend, Adrian, and crying 'TEARS of joy' for what he had just accomplished. He was a rank outsider, with seemingly no chance of lasting more than a couple of rounds with Apollo Creed, yet he made it through fifteen. So, how did he do it? Was it talent? Was it strength? Was it luck? Was it because Sylvester Stallone wrote the script? Well, actually, yes, it was that last one! However, in the movie, Rocky got to that 'TEARS of joy' moment because of a thought he focused on many months earlier.

In this book, I want you to know, believe, and practice a basic concept. Every thought counts and, with the power of faith, every thought, belief, or perspective starts a domino-type effect that will lead to an outcome. That outcome will either be one you love, and may lead to 'TEARS of joy', or one that you hate, and possibly lead to *tears of pain*. It all depends on your thought, belief, or perspective. Whether you have a Christian faith or not, I want to teach you about the simple and predictable process to experience 'TEARS of joy' repeatedly in your life. If that sounds good to you, then this is the book for you. So, keep reading...

CHAPTER 1

'TEARS of Joy'

*"Nothing will happen in your life without
a strong emotion to drive it."*

Can you think of times in your life when you pushed to achieve something important, overcame something that was weighing on you, fixed a valuable relationship, or came to a startling realisation and, without even knowing why, tears were uncontrollably pouring out of your eyes? They are 'TEARS of joy'! They represent a release of powerful emotion after a success, a breakthrough, or an occurrence that perhaps, at some stage, didn't seem possible. They symbolise something so important to you that the meaning of the outcome is far greater than words can ever describe. These tears demonstrate unconditional love, burning desire, incredible relief, or the joy of achievement, and will always say more than any words ever could.

I am a crier! What can I say? I am extremely sensitive. So sensitive, in fact, I have been caught crying watching a heart-warming episode of the *Brady Bunch*. Please keep that embarrassing admission under your hat. Thanks. It's not good for my manly image! I love watching movies based on true stories. I often find myself crying 'TEARS of joy' as the amazing achievement depicted in the story comes to fruition.

If you have ever watched the movie *October Sky*, you will know what I am talking about. I think, conservatively, I've watched it fifteen times. I can say without fear of contradiction or judgement, I have cried at the end, every single time. It's based on the true story of a teenager named Homer Hickham, living in a small mining town in Virginia, USA, in the 1950s. Everyone in this town has pretty much resigned themselves to the fact they will end up working in the mines, except Homer. He decides, after seeing the Russian satellite, *Sputnik*, in 1957 speed across the October sky, that he was going to build a rocket and go into space.

Ironically, his father is the boss of the mine and expects his son to follow in his footsteps. Much of the movie is about Homer and his three friends building a rocket, winning first place at the USA Science Fair, and getting scholarships to university. It is also about the strained and often volatile relationship with his father, who is very strong, opinionated, and critical. Homer does everything he can to try and convince his father that mining is not for him. He wants to follow his dream and go into space. However, his father won't accept this and almost disowns him.

Homer, like all children, just wants his father's attention and approval and continually invites him to come and watch the firing of his rockets. Unfortunately, his father, John, is always too busy. With each rejection by his father, you can see the heartbreaking look on Homer's face. However, there is a point in the movie in which the penny finally drops for John Hickham. After Homer had won first place in the science fair – and, without even realising it, met a man he really respected, Dr Werner Von Braun – he is back in Coalwood. The following conversation with his dad is a turning point and where my tears begin to well up.

Homer: *We're shooting off our last rocket today at 5 o'clock if you'd like to come and see it.*

John: *I've got a lot of work to do.*

Homer, with a disappointed look on his face: *Oh, okay, just thought I'd ask.*

John: *Hear you met your big hero. Didn't even know it.*

Homer: *Look. I know you and me don't exactly see eye to eye on certain things. I mean, man, we don't see eye to eye on just about anything. But I've come to believe that I got it in me to be somebody in this world. And it's not because I'm so different from you either. It's 'cause I'm the same. I can be just as hard-headed and just as tough. I only hope I can be as good a man as you are. I mean, sure, Dr Von Braun's a great scientist, but he isn't my hero.*

At that moment, as Homer walks away, you can see the impact on his father's face. Later that day, Homer and *the rocket boys* are getting ready to shoot off their last rocket. The crowd has grown as Homer longingly looks around to see if his father is in attendance. He isn't. So, Homer thanks people who helped, and, as he is about to finish speaking and is thanking his mother <u>and</u> father, his dad appears. It's hard to describe this scene without watching it, but I can tell you that every time I watch it and see the look on Homer's face when his dad pushes through the crowd, I dissolve into a flood of tears. I mean every time, and I've seen it many times! It is such a heart-warming and joyous ending that it gets me in tears every single time.

Where do these tears come from? They come from a build-up of desire, effort, struggle, persistence and, finally, achievement, or break-through. They are an indication of what that achievement and fulfilment really means in your life. Some people, however, achieve things that don't result in tears.

When I graduated from my four-year tertiary degree, I was glad it was over but not so joy-filled that it warranted the spilling of eye water. When I got my first job as a teacher, I think there were some tears, but maybe more because I was sad I had a job, or maybe because I got something in my eye! In this book, I am talking about real tears. These are the tears that come from a place deep in your heart and deep in your desires. Tears mean you are heading in the direction of your destiny and towards your purpose in life.

My first 'TEARS of joy' moment came when I was maybe four years old, as I stood next to my mother while she was ironing. I had my own mini-iron and ironing board, and I was doing the ironing with her. Yes, I had an iron and ironing board! What can I say? I was an attention-seeking, middle-child mama's boy! As I looked up at her, she looked at me with love and pride in her eyes, and I felt it. The 'TEARS of joy' came from the love I felt from my mother.

As a sixteen-year-old, I experienced 'TEARS of joy' when I received an invitation to train at the St Kilda Football Club, a professional foot-ball club in Melbourne, Australia. It was something that I had been working hard towards for several years, and until that day, I wasn't sure whether it was possible for me. The tears came as incredible joy and pride in what I had achieved to that point.

As I mentioned, I'm a crier. I cried when I was selected for my first under 19s game and first reserves game. When I was selected for my first senior game, I absolutely sobbed. I cried when I published my first book and every book after that! I cry watching great movies where there is an inspiring and happy ending. As I admitted earlier, I have even cried watching the *Brady Bunch*! It means I'm a passionate and emotional person. I will tell you from personal experience, nothing will happen in your life without a strong emotion to drive it. This is a fact we will get into more detail about as we progress through the book.

One of the most meaningful, emotional, and tearful times in my life occurred relatively recently. It was when, after some turmoil and uncertainty in my life, a trusted friend and mentor suggested that a relationship with God may be what I need. If it were anyone else's suggestion, I probably would have disregarded it. However, after she explained the impact it had on her life, I was intrigued. So, I explored, decided I had nothing to lose, and accepted Jesus Christ as my saviour. Let me tell you this. Whether you are a sceptic or not, the feeling of faith, the knowledge that I am forgiven of my poor choices and mistakes, and to feel the freedom that comes from a belief that I am divinely guided was, and is, powerful. So many incredibly freeing 'TEARS of joy' moments have occurred since that time, just a few years ago.

Have a think about something that has resulted in 'TEARS of joy' for you. When you think about it, does it get the tears flowing again, or at least produce a lump in your throat, a smile on your face, and a warm feeling in your heart? Now, I want you to think about the effort involved, the struggles, the challenges, and the persistence it took to get to the 'TEARS of joy' stage. Are you amazed at how you did it? I am, often. I always pinch myself and check that it's real and not a dream that I played professional sport and am now a full-time author, and loving my life. It's not a life without challenges, insecurities, and struggles, but a life I love, nevertheless. What about you?

Whilst many things seem unlikely, even impossible, when you follow a predictable set of rules, you will get an equally predictable result, no matter how unlikely it may seem. I am living proof of that, as I call myself an *unlikely athlete* and *accidental author*. You may not have journaled, planned, or even remembered the process that got you to the point of joyful tears. However, it would create an equally amazing result if repeated with other things in your life. I never deliberately followed a predictable plan to play senior professional football. Looking back, I can see that it fits the rules I will share with you in this book. I never had a ten-point plan to become a successful published author. I can see that the process I followed intuitively was the right one to allow me to get that result and experience more 'TEARS of joy'.

So, get excited about the journey you are on the verge of undertaking. As you read the pages of this book, many things will feel familiar to you because you have already implemented many of the processes I will discuss. You just may not have been conscious of it or realised they were the right actions to take. I want to formalise and systemise predictable success for you. I hope that you will use it, time and time again, to experience 'TEARS of joy' in your life as often as possible. It is my passion to help you live a purposeful life of joyful longevity.

Moving towards 'TEARS of Joy'

> Romans 15:13 – *May the God of hope fill you with all joy and peace as you trust in Him, so that you may overflow with hope by the power of the Holy Spirit.* (NIV)

In this world, at this moment in time, many people are floating along in life, just taken by the current without any idea where they are heading or why. It is a tragedy because we were put on this planet for a reason. We all have a destiny. We all have unique talents and abilities. But, most importantly, we all have a deep-down dream, desire, and purpose just bursting to get out. Unfortunately, the reality for many people is they have pushed that dream and purpose so far down for so long, they have forgotten they are amazing humans and are on this planet to make a difference. If that is you, I hope this book wakes you up and helps you drag your dreams and desires back up to see the light of day.

The moment you can get some clarity about what you want and become emotionally attached to its fulfilment, you will automatically engage a process that, with some focus, persistence, and belief, will lead you to the point where many more 'TEARS of joy' will start flooding from your eyes. Stick with me throughout this book because it is about you. If you give up reading this book and stop acting on the suggestions, you will effectively give up on yourself and your own dreams. Hang in there. It is so worth it!

Key questions and action steps

1. Think about times in your life when you experienced 'TEARS of joy'.
2. What had you achieved or what had happened?
3. Why were there tears, and what did those tears represent?
4. What was the process you went through to get to the point when those tears flowed?
5. What is something you are striving for right now that would bring 'TEARS of joy' once achieved?
6. Are you ready to start a plan to create an exciting reality?
7. If yes, great, keep reading.

CHAPTER 2

Understanding the TEARS acronym

"The TEARS, in 'TEARS of joy', is an acronym and a formula for a process to predictably achieve your own happiness and success."

Many people look at the success of others and wonder why those people are so fortunate. They then look at their own circumstances and dwell on the reasons why they are so unlucky. The great news, and potentially the confronting news, is that whatever situation you are dealing with in your life – good or bad – you created it. Therefore, you can take full credit for your successes – that's the good news. However, you must also take full responsibility for the negative outcomes in your life – that is clearly a bitter pill to swallow. Now, I'm not saying you are responsible for all the adversity in your life. However, you are absolutely in control of how you respond, react, and deal with that adversity.

If you were to look at the success or lack of success of two people and track it backwards, you would find that the very same formula, process, or system was in play. It's never luck, age, background, financial position, health, or any of the other things many people will offer as an excuse for their lack of success. To put it simply, their lack of success is due to putting the wrong information into their computer. That computer is their brain.

I'm sure you own a car, or you know someone who does. On a regular basis, you need to put fuel, oil, and water in that car for it to function effectively. Right? Now let's say two people purchased the same car on the same day and bought it brand new. The first owner was meticulous about their new car. The car was serviced regularly, only high-quality fuel was used, the best oil available went into the car, and the water kept at the optimal level. The second owner was not nearly as focused on maintaining their new car. The car was rarely serviced, the lowest grade fuel was used, the cheapest oil was only put in the car when desperate, and the car often overheated. What is the result or performance of these two cars? It's not hard to answer that question, is it?

The first owner will have a car that drives well, lasts longer, and gives a great performance. The second owner will have ongoing problems and may even blame the manufacturer for the car's lack of longevity. The reality is that they both started with the same cars, the same engines, and the same potential. However, because they put different things into their respective engines, they got totally different outcomes. Same engine, or the same system, but because of the input, the output was predictable. The same can be said about you and the things you achieve in your life, and whether you experience 'TEARS of joy' or *tears of regret*.

In my book, *Dance Until it Rains*, I talk about my greatest hero, my mother, Sue. I want to share two similar scenarios she faced, with two entirely different outcomes. The idea here is that you will be firmly convinced that, in most cases, you are in control of your destiny by what you put into your mental engine. In 1988, my mother was diagnosed with breast cancer which was medically treated and removed. In 1989, she was diagnosed with secondary liver cancer. I believe she was diagnosed with liver cancer less than eighteen months after the breast cancer diagnosis because of how she reacted to the initial diagnosis and the most predominant thoughts in her mind.

In 1988, she was a busy mother, wife, librarian, and friend who thought life was going along as it should. Her world, in fact, the world of her whole family, was rocked to the core when she was diagnosed with breast cancer. She had no idea how to respond, so I believe the way she reacted was predictable, and like most people would have reacted. In her mind, it was not fair, and it was bad luck. Unfortunately, she didn't look at her beliefs and habits that may have contributed to this diagnosis and focus on changing those. Instead, she reacted with fear, a victim mindset and helplessness, which led her to simply presenting herself to the conventional medical profession to be fixed. In their defence, doctors did the best they could, based on their understanding and education. They treated her surgically, chemically, and synthetically, just not holistically. After treatment and time, they seemed confident they had eliminated cancer from her body and gave her the all-clear.

However, what had not been eliminated were the reasons why cancer presented, and why she was diagnosed in the first place. She didn't change the negative thoughts, the fear and anxiety she was still carrying, or any other activities that could potentially cause a recurrence. She kept smoking, eating the way she had always done, and held onto issues from her childhood. Looking back now, as devastating as it appeared at the time, it was not surprising that secondary liver cancer emerged less than eighteen months later. When it did, the prognosis from the doctors, due to their educated and considered opinion, was that if she lasted three years, she would be lucky.

This time, however, my mother put a considerably different input into her mental engine. She became angry and determined. Angry that she didn't take more responsibility the first time and determined she would do everything in her power to return to optimal health. She refused to be solely influenced by the doctor's gloomy prediction, specially since they had been so horribly wrong with their initial declaration that the cancer was gone. This decision set off a chain reaction of thoughts, emotions, actions, and habits that, in her specific situation, helped turn a three-year death sentence into a fifteen-year journey of happiness, abundance, well-being, and many 'TEARS of joy'. Tragically, she passed away many years earlier than we all wanted. I often ask the question, if she had taken this positive and holistic approach to the diagnosis of the initial breast cancer, would she still be here? She lived a wonderful life, although shortened, and is an inspiring example of the process I am about to share with you.

In 'TEARS of joy', the TEARS is an acronym and a formula for a process to predictably achieve your own success, and experience your own 'TEARS of joy' as often as you choose. Be aware this same acronym and process can also lead to *tears of pain*, depending on what you feed your brain at the beginning of the journey. Just like the car being mistreated and fuelled with the cheapest fuel, and my mother feeding her thoughts with a negative and victim mentality. Are you ready to find out what TEARS stands for? I'm sure you already know it, but here it is anyway:

THOUGHT

EMOTION

ROUTINE

SUCCESS

I want to talk from a positive, goal achievement and 'TEARS of joy' point of view, where the 'S' stands for Success. If you put in the wrong thought focus at the beginning of this process, you will discover it will lead to a broken car, a sick body, an unhappy mind, an empty bank account, or a lonely person. In this case, the 'S' certainly doesn't stand for success. It would probably represent any or all of sick, sad, sinking, scarce, self-destruct, shattered, sluggish, sorrowful, stressed, suffering, or any other yucky 's' adjectives you can think of. Okay, let's now shake off those horrible words, and stay focused on the process that will absolutely lead you to success, and the 'TEARS of joy' you are deserving of, and destined for.

It's vital to realise that every outcome you and I experience in any area of our life is largely our own doing. Yep, sorry about that. I know it's not what you want to hear, but it's what you and I need to hear. The reason is that every outcome, good or bad, happy or sad, and successful or sinking, starts with a single and simple **thought,** belief, or perspective that you choose to focus on. That thought is either positive and empowering or negative and disempowering. Think about a specific result you are currently getting in your life, and spend some time reflecting on your thoughts, beliefs, ideas, and attitudes towards it. Later in this chapter, I describe a real-life example of this process that I recently experienced in a Christian college as I was talking to a group of thirteen and fourteen-year-old students.

The thought we choose to focus on, or change, will then lead to **emotion** or **emotions**, which will be based on the orientation of the thought. In my mother's example, when diagnosed with breast cancer, she focused on disempowering thoughts. *Why me? It's not fair. I don't want to die.* These thoughts lead to emotions of fear, anger, helplessness, and despair. On the other hand, when the secondary cancer was detected, she decided to take control and be proactive, which led to determination, optimism, and hope. The emotions then, very much, determined what she did next. It is our emotions, which drive our actions. In fact, the word emotion could be written as e-motion and be expanded to **explain-motion, excite-motion** or even **agitate-motion.** Yes, I know agitate doesn't start with an 'e', but it's a cool word.

So, emotion is a key factor in the immediate **actions** we take. When you are angry or upset, you may do or say something you later regret. Ever done that? I know I have. When you are experiencing an empowering emotion, you are more likely to do and say things that will keep those strong emotions happening and moving you towards a successful outcome. Throughout the book, I will expand on how our emotions significantly impact our physical health and explain the unexplainable. For example, how my 97-year-old Hungarian great-grandmother smoked a carton of cigarettes every week, drank brandy every day, ate rich Hungarian food, yet lived a long and happy life.

If a positive emotion leads to a positive action, which reinforces the positive emotion that leads to the same positive actions, then over time, with focus and attention, you will develop positive and powerful habits or **routines.** The same is true for negative emotion and actions. We all have habits and routines, some good and some not so good. Interestingly, good habits tend to take more deliberate time, energy, and focus. Yet, the bad habits just seem to occur without any thought or attention at all. Have you ever noticed that?

Make no mistake about it. The life you live, the joy you experience, the things you achieve, and your **success** is almost always due to your established habits and routines. As you reflect on your past aspirations and results, you will know this is true for you. Just to make sure you are clear, every outcome you experience, and will experience in life, is the result of your unconscious routines.

So, in summary, your **success** in life comes down to these **routines**, which come from repeating the right **actions** inspired by your **emotions** which you control because of the **thoughts** you choose to focus on. Follow this process, and the result will predictably be 'TEARS of joy'.

Several years ago, I was divinely led to pick up and read a book called *The Magic is in the Extra Mile* by Larry Di Angi. As a logical thinking fitness professional, I believed that exercise, nutrition, and sleep were the most important things that determined longevity and well-being. As a result of God's guidance to read that book, my thinking radically changed for the better when I studied three short paragraphs at the beginning:

> A national news program conducted a study of fifty people who have lived over 100 years and still lead active, happy lives. The researchers specifically looked for similarities in diet, exercise, lifestyle, and habits that could contribute to their longevity and quality of life. What they found was amazing.

> We are becoming more and more aware of the great benefits of a healthy diet and exercise, and the researchers expected to find these factors to be the major contributors. Through an extensive interviewing process, the news team found that some of the participants in this study had what would be considered good diets. An equal number of people were not as healthy in their food choices. Exercise and other areas of lifestyle were also not found to be a common thread throughout the group.

> However, two things were overwhelmingly consistent among over 90% of those studied. What were these consistent traits? Nine out of ten said that throughout their

entire lives they awoke every morning with an *attitude of gratitude* for one more day of life and they saw each day as a precious gift. Secondly, nine out of ten stated that they felt that life was too short to hold grudges or spend time complaining, and they forgave people quickly and refused to dwell on negative thoughts.

In reading this, my thinking about what represented optimal well-being and longevity dramatically changed. These joyful and active 100-plusers chose to control and direct their thoughts, beliefs, and perspectives. The focus on thoughts that led to gratitude, forgiveness and positivity started the wonderful domino effect on their emotions, actions, and routines. The result being their wonderful success as they surpassed that magical 100-year mark and were active, happy, and valuable. Powerful stuff!

Not long ago, I spoke to a group of thirteen and fourteen-year-old students at a well-known Christian college in Melbourne. I talked about 'TEARS of joy' and discussed the process from **T**hought to **E**motion to **A**ction to **R**outine to **S**uccess. Then I asked them to do a simple activity. I handed out a sheet that looked like this...

Andrew Jobling
ANDREWJOBLING.COM.AU

Creating TEARS of Joy

SUCCESS _____

ROUTINE ···························

EMOTION _____

THOUGHT _____

I started by asking each student to fill in the **S**uccess section by writing down one thing that represented success for them. Something they would like to achieve by the end of the year. I then asked if any students would be willing to share what they had written. Four young people put their hands up. I made sure all the other students knew they needed to encourage and support the dreams and aspirations of these few teenagers who had to courage to publicly declare them. Three of the students had reasonably predictable goals: win an academic award, write a book, and make the sporting team. The fourth boy stood up, and after I asked him what he wanted to achieve by the end of the year, in front of more than 200 students, he said: "I want to get better grades because I am dumb".

All the talking stopped, and all the eyes looked at me. Right then, God spoke to me to let me know this was a perfect opportunity, with this student, to illustrate what I was talking about. I asked him: "When you <u>think</u> you're dumb, how does it make <u>you feel</u>?" He replied briefly, as only a fourteen-year-old boy can: "Sad, bad and discouraged". I then worked through the model with him and asked: "Believing you are dumb and feeling the way you do, what <u>actions</u> do you normally take regarding your school-work?" His answer was predictable: "I don't do much because I'm dumb, so, what's the point?" Then I asked: "So, what study <u>routine</u> do you have?" He looked at me, smiled a sheepish smile, and though he didn't need to say any more, he replied: "None really. I get home, watch some TV, play computer games, and go to bed." The results he was achieving had nothing to do with his ability and everything to do with non-action. His thinking that he was dumb had a powerful ripple effect that impacted his results.

I then asked him: "Do you want to get better grades?" He said: "Yes". I asked him: "Are you willing to work to improve?" He said: "Yes". I then asked him: "Are you willing to start today?" He said: "Yes". Then I told him: "You are not dumb. In fact, you are one of the smartest people I know. Intelligence is not a reflection of what you know. It's all about what you do."

From that point, we refined and clarified his goal and **Success** to <u>achieve a B in Science</u>. Again, working through the sheet he had, I asked him what study **Routine** he would need and be willing to develop. He said he would spend time each day, for at least thirty minutes, on improving his Science. I asked him what **Action** he would be willing to take today. He told me he would ask his science teacher what she recommended, and do his first thirty minutes that evening. I asked him what **Emotion** he would experience when he achieved that B in Science. His face lit up as he told me he would feel proud, excited, and happy. I then asked what his **Thought** was now about his ability to achieve that result in science. He said: "I can and will do it. I can work and improve and achieve any result I want."

Wow! Do you understand the significance of what happened that day? It seems like a simple, even insignificant conversation but just think about what just occurred for that fourteen-year-old. If he continued to think and believe he was dumb, what path would he be on? He would probably continue to apply minimal effort and get poor results. He would potentially develop a behavioural problem, leave school early, and fall into the wrong crowd. What about now? Knowing, thinking, and believing that he can work, improve, and achieve any result he wants? Where will he end up? I truly hope he follows through because anything is possible for that courageous young man.

Moving towards 'TEARS of Joy'

> Philippians 4:8 – *Finally, brothers and sisters, whatever is true, whatever is noble, whatever is right, whatever is pure, whatever is lovely, whatever is admirable – if anything is excellent or praiseworthy – think about such things.* (NIV)

Why do we complicate life when it is quite simple? We are often too quick to look outside of ourselves for the answers to questions that are happily residing in the six inches between our ears. Suppose we know and believe every outcome we experience in life begins with a thought we choose to focus on. And that the right thought will initiate a domino effect to deliver us everything we want. Would we be more deliberate about our thoughts, and would our world be a different place? If we could be more deliberate about what we allow to enter and stay in our minds, we would be happier, healthier, wealthier, and more successful in every area of our lives.

In the following chapters, I will unpack each piece of this simple formula to help you predictably create success and 'TEARS of joy' in any and every area of your life that is important to you. Just know, as you move forward through this book, everything you have and will have is because of your thoughts. Start now to become aware of the thoughts and words that are normal and natural for you. They are the current predictor of the direction you are heading in life.

Key questions and action steps

1. Think about times in your life when there were 'TEARS of joy'. Why? What was the process you went through?
2. They say that a change is as good as a holiday. Are you ready for a change in your life?
3. If you answered yes, please spend the next couple of days being very conscious of your thoughts and whether they are mostly negative or positive in their orientation?
4. Are you ready and willing to spend the time to change any negative and limiting thoughts and beliefs, even if they are very firmly established? I hope so.
5. Keep reading and enjoy.

CHAPTER 3

Finding my faith – A 'TEARS of joy' transformation

"If I want an exceptional life, and I do, I need to do exceptional things. Prayer, belief in Jesus and a relationship with God is one way I am fulfilling this wonderful life."

At this stage of the book, I think it's important to share something about me, my journey, and my transformation over the last few years. One that has helped me find peace, purpose and many wonderful 'TEARS of joy' moments. To be completely honest, and whilst on paper, my achievements and life look like a success, I have struggled in many areas of my life for many years. It wasn't until a trusted friend and mentor suggested something to me that changed everything. Please understand my only intention in telling you my story is to give you the complete picture and to help you make the best decisions for your own life.

As an author, mentor, and speaker, I am torn between a desire to be seen as having my life together and being open and vulnerable about the insecurities and struggles I go through every day. The reality is, for much of my life, I have lived with insecurity, fear, and anxiety. Why?

I'm not sure. I was born into a loving family and had all the support, encouragement, and opportunity that a boy could want or need. Maybe it was the unspoken burden that my mother passed onto me after a lifetime of her own challenges, struggles, insecurity and feeling that she was never good enough.

My mother has since passed away but is always in my heart. She has left a wonderful legacy that will live on in many lives. Her early days shaped the fearful little girl she was, influenced the adult she became, and may well be responsible for the insecurity she carried through much of her life. That was, until the diagnosis of secondary liver cancer, at the age of 54, when she decided enough was enough. That decision helped her reconcile many thoughts, feelings, and perspectives she had harboured for decades before she started to genuinely love and value herself. Watching my mother's transformation and how it helped her outlive a cancer prognosis by fifteen years inspires me every day. In fact, the thoughts and decisions in her life at that time were the catalyst for many 'TEARS of joy' moments, some of which I explore in this book.

My mother was born in Budapest, Hungary, in 1935. There is no need for me to reveal her entire story. However, I hope what I do share will give you the context for a timid little boy filled with insecurity, fear, and feelings that he was never good enough. That timid little boy was me. My mother's mother and her family were Jewish. I don't think I need to explain why it was dangerous for them to be in Europe at that time in history. My grandparents had amazing foresight to observe the political, social, and religious unrest brewing in Hungary and Europe. In 1939 they decided to leave Hungary and find a better life for their small family. My mother was an only child at the time.

While my grandparents had amazing strength and courage to make a move to Australia, they lacked the skills to comfort a scared four-year-old and help her feel safe and loved. From a young age, my mother was, in many ways, treated like an adult way before she was mature enough or ready to take on and understand those responsibilities. Her parents, distracted and dealing with their own uncertainty and fears, found communicating effectively with their first-born daughter difficult. My mother was expected to handle a move across the world at the age of four. As a child, she was expected to help at home and in the new family business. Unfairly, she effectively became a second mother when her sister and brother came along eight and ten years after her own birth.

From a young age, and understandably so, my mother developed a belief that she had to work to earn love, and that she was not loved unconditionally. She held this belief during her childhood and teenage years and into her young adult life. She also carried this belief into her marriage and with her children until she felt worthy, unconditionally loved, and ready to fight a cancer diagnosis. As a small child, I was very much a mama's boy and extremely attached to my mother. I was also sensitive to her own fear and insecurities. Consequently, as I try to do some self-analysis of my psychological issues, I believe I absorbed those feelings, which was a large part of the reason why I was a timid, shy, and insecure child.

As a result of my own feelings of insecurity, I craved attention and validation. For much of my life, I have been a chaser of things I could never catch. As a young child, I chased attention through showing off and, at times, needy behaviour. It never helped me feel better about myself. In my teens and early twenties, I chased fame and recognition as a professional athlete, believing it would help me feel better about myself. While I am incredibly proud of my achievements, it didn't ease the emptiness I felt inside. When I started working in the health and fitness industry, I invested vast amounts of time and effort into my body. I believed that having a body people admired would help me love myself more. Again, I am glad I focused on my health and fitness, as I still do today. However, my athletic and impressive external body never eased the feelings of insecurity bubbling away under the surface.

Even my decision to write my first book was because I believed that, if I were a known, admired, and respected published author, I would feel better about myself. Do you know what? Becoming an author did help me feel that I was able to impact the lives of others. It did help with my confidence in many respects, but the elusive self-love I was chasing just seemed to keep getting further and further away. Then, there are my relationships!

In mid-2019, my eleven-year marriage ended. It was my third marriage. Again, my life journey with relationships had been fuelled by a desperate desire to feel loved and accepted. In all my relationships, even though my partners gave me what I thought I wanted, it still wasn't enough. Why? Because what I was chasing could never be provided by another person. Over the years, there were many tears in my relationships, some were of joy, but many were not. There were *tears of anger* (largely with me), *tears of sadness*, *tears of regret*, *tears of heartbreak*, *tears of frustration*, and even *tears of hopelessness*.

This continual need for validation and acceptance meant I was not giving my partner or my relationship the attention it deserved. I'm not going to go into detail about what happened. Needless to say, my marriage hit a crisis point, and I knew I was the primary source of the problem. I just didn't know how to change or resolve this empty feeling in my heart. On the surface, and from an external viewpoint, things seemed to be going so well. I had a gorgeous wife, was a successful author and speaker, was lean, fit, and healthy, and I looked like I had everything sorted. I made it seem that way, but the reality was that everything was balanced on a razor's edge because, spiritually, I was empty.

I didn't know what to believe in. I had always been taught to treat people well. I semi-believed that the universe delivered what I needed. I had always lived by the Aussie mantra, *she'll be right, mate.* Well, let me tell you, *she* most definitely was not right at that point of my life, mate. I was not loving myself at all. My marriage was hanging by the thinnest of threads. I was not clear on my purpose in life. I was just surviving financially, and I was stressed, anxious, and fearful. I am so grateful for a trusted friend and mentor who suggested a way I could get through this. I was at a desperate point in my life and was willing to try pretty much anything.

My friend had been on her own spiritual journey after a marriage breakdown and a personal health scare when she found Christianity. She explained that a relationship with God and building her own faith provided answers. Her faith helped her to let go of some guilt and shame, helped her forgive herself and others, and brought an incredible level of peace and meaning to her life. I mean, come on, who wouldn't want that? At that point in my life, tears were commonplace, just not 'TEARS of joy'. As I mentioned earlier, they were *tears of sadness, tears of shame, tears of regret,* and *tears of anger.*

As I will discuss, the tears you and I experience, in most cases, are the predictable result of the same process. This is whether they are 'TEARS of joy' after a meaningful event or successful achievement, or *tears of pain* after trauma or an undesirable episode. The only difference between 'TEARS of joy' and *tears of pain* is the thought, perspective, or belief we focus on that start the domino effect. It was certainly the case for me as I reflected on my journey through my marriage and life crisis at that time.

On my friend's recommendation, my wife and I flew to New South Wales to attend a week-long Christian healing event run by Art Mathias. To say I felt like a fish out of water was the understatement of the year. Up until that time, I had spent no time focusing on God, or that the life and death of Jesus could release me and save me from the poor choices of my past, and guide me through the uncertainty of my future. When I was at school, I tolerated religious studies but paid no attention to the words, messages, or meaning in my life. I enjoyed Christmas and Easter holidays without any focus on their significance and Christian meaning.

I tolerated going to church for weddings, funerals, and baptisms just to get the celebration on the other side.

Now, I was in a week-long Christian seminar focused very much on the healing and forgiving word of God, and I felt incredibly uncomfortable. I knew, however, I needed to be uncomfortable at that time in my life if things were going to change. The first few days were just about understanding what was going on, and what was really being said. It was also about trying to rid myself of the scepticism I had about the power of God and the miracles that faith in his word could create. It wasn't that, at the time, I didn't believe in God. I just didn't have any evidence to support it or really understand the power of faith.

Over the week, I watched Art Mathias work with people who had experienced incredible trauma in their lives. People who had lived with the shame, guilt, pain, and the many repercussions of abuse of all types. Some people had been the victims, and some had been the perpetrators. No matter what they had done or experienced, there was healing and forgiveness available to them. These were people whose lives were in a mess, far worse than the mess my life was in, that's for sure. I watched Art move people through the forgiveness and healing phase and helped them access the healing and forgiving power of God. I watched transformation after transformation in front of my eyes. Did I honestly believe it? No, I don't think I did at that time, but I was intrigued, and I was open to exploring.

By the end of the week, I got to a stage where I needed to spill my guts to Art and explain the hurt I felt inside. I finally felt comfortable enough to share, and safe enough that he could help me without judgement. I told him where I was at in my life and my marriage, and why we were at the event. I spoke about my actions, my shame, and my concerns about losing my wife. He listened with compassion, and then we prayed the two prayers we had learned during the week, the repentance prayer and the forgiveness prayer.

You know what? I immediately felt some peace in my heart. Something I hadn't felt for a long time. I didn't really understand how or why, and I didn't really believe any more, but it was enough to intrigue me. If this could help me in my life, then why wouldn't I explore it? I was still unsure, however, a little sceptical and absolutely terrified of venturing down a Christian path. I was unsure whether it would hold the answers I was looking for. I was sceptical because the miracles that were spoken about, and the immediacy of the impact, was still hard to get my head around. I was scared about how I may be seen and what others would think of me, specially my reading and listening audience.

In fact, even now, as I am writing this part of the book, I am concerned the non-Christian readers will miss what I am trying to say here and miss the value and insights this book offers. It is important to realise I am just telling my story. I am not preaching or pressuring. I know you are intelligent, and I know you will read this with an open heart and an open mind and act on information you believe is relevant to your life. You will know if it can help you move forward to experience 'TEARS of joy' repeatedly.

Let me tell you, I went home from that week-long Christian seminar with hope, relief, gratitude, and peace. I felt hope that everything would be okay, relief that I didn't need to have all the answers and gratitude that I was forgiven. I felt peace because I started to believe that I would be okay, whatever happened in my life and marriage. It was the beginning of a journey for me that I am grateful for every day. Not an easy journey, by any stretch of the imagination, but a journey that has and will continue to bring 'TEARS of joy' moments into my life.

As I got home from the week away, I was determined to find a church to attend and start trying to get my head around Christianity. I will admit, it was a challenge for me. Mostly because much of my life and the things I have achieved have been very dependent on faith. It was just not a faith that included God or a saviour. I soon found a church and started to attend each week, thinking that it would make more sense. Ha! It got even more confusing and confronting for me than in the beginning. The people were friendlier than I was comfortable with, I did not understand much of the Bible, and I just had a hard time understanding the foundation of Christianity.

That God sent his only son to Earth to live and then be crucified was a challenge for me. That His body was broken, so I would be healed, and His blood shed so that I would be forgiven of my sins, I could not understand. That if I believed Jesus died on the cross for me, and if I declared him the saviour of my life, I would have eternal life, was very confusing. When you come from fifty-plus years of thinking and believing one way, it is hard to take such a dramatic and confronting hairpin turn. I loved everything Christianity stood for in terms of forgiveness, freedom, healing, and miracles. I just didn't get it. If I am being honest, I still do not totally get it. The difference now is that I have experienced so many blessings due to this correction in my life.

Over the last few years, and with some challenging situations, my life has moved to another level of forgiveness. This includes joy, fulfilment, achievement, and most importantly, self-love. My transition into a relationship with God and being baptised as a born-again Christian has played a profound part in that. Am I perfect? Far from it. But the most important feeling I have now is trust. I trust God that I am forgiven and that my path is divinely guided.

I have learned to forgive myself, even for my poor choices, the people I have impacted, and the mistakes I have made. I am focused on reading the Bible every day, even though I do not always understand it. I feel a greater level of peace and certainty about my path and purpose with each waking moment. I can face challenges with excitement and the expectation that God has a plan. Each circumstance will lead me to destiny, why I was created and what I was put on this planet for.

As I mentioned, I found myself single again in my mid-fifties, which was never a part of my plan. I was left with a huge hole in my heart, home, and life. Being alone was never something I was good at because I didn't like myself for most of my life. I would do anything not to be alone. At that time in my life, I knew things needed to be different than the way they were before, or else I would continue to follow the same patterns that led me there in the first place. The main pattern I became aware of was to rush into the next relationship without reconciling the last relationship or the way I felt about myself. From painful personal experience, let me tell you that that is not a solution or a pattern to fall into.

I knew there were two relationships I had to develop before I could possibly consider another romantic connection. One was with God; the other was with me. I spoke to God every day, I prayed, I repented, and I asked for His unconditional love and forgiveness. In my heart, I felt He was there and loving me, despite my flaws. Let me tell you, this was and is a game-changer for me. But boy, being alone was hard work, and so often I was tempted to fall back into my own pattern. Even talking to God could not repress that strong pull back into old ways. Then, just when I was about to give in to the enemy's hold on me, the best possible thing happened in my life.

As I write this chapter, it is the second half of 2021, and, as I look back at my 2020, I will say something that may be controversial to some. I certainly don't mean it disrespectfully to anyone who has experienced any suffering or loss during that time. I am very empathetic to those people. In my situation, I have to say the best thing that has happened in my life for a long time is the global COVID pandemic and the world going into lockdown. Yes, I told you that sounds weird and a little controversial but let me explain. In many ways, I am a better person, I have a stronger faith, I can make more of a difference. I have a global audience and am connected with some incredible people. Most importantly, I have re-built the most important relationship I have – the one with myself.

The uncertainty of this COVID-19 time has opened the door to many opportunities to simply trust that God is looking out for me and helping me live on purpose.

My future speaking and mentoring uncertainty opened the possibility of other ways to help and communicate, helping me move from a local market to a global one. I am a much bigger thinker and have met, and am now collaborating, with winners worldwide. It wouldn't have happened without the uncertainty of this time. I started my podcast, which I am loving, and I know it's making a difference. I doubt whether it would have happened without the lockdown and the uncertainty that came with it. I found more people to help write their books, improve their wellbeing, and enhance their financial position. Without the uncertainty of this time, I don't think these opportunities would have been a possibility. Most importantly, the uncertainty of lockdown and isolation has created the most amazing outcome, that is, to take the time to get to know, like, and even love me. What an absolute gift from God!

In this time, I have developed a routine that I know has brought me many 'TEARS of joy', some *tears of relief*, and some *tears of release* and *freedom*. My weekly connection to my church and the community has given me a place I feel at home. Even during the lockdown period, the online community has grown and helped immensely. The friends I have made within the church are people who, I know, will be friends for life. The way I can use my lessons, stories, and experience to add value to the Christian community excites me. This book is part of that.

Every morning after my training, I pray to God. Now let me tell you this was a challenging routine to start, and I struggled with what to say, how to say it, and what to ask for. Then I went to a worship session and heard a speaker talk about how he prays. He uses the word PRAY as an acronym for **P**raise, **R**epent, **A**sk and **Y**ield. I thought to myself, I can do that. Each morning I **praise** God for what he has done and is doing in the world and my life. Then, I **repent** for poor choices and mistakes, ask for forgiveness, and forgive myself. Next, I unashamedly **ask** for stuff. I ask for the healing of the suffering, for sick people and, specifically, people I know need help. I ask for the wisdom and courage to become a better person and for opportunities to help more people and get my message out to the world. I ask for help to find my soul mate. I ask for an abundance of money, time, health, love, and joy. Then I **yield** to him.

After my prayer session, I take my fluffy little girl, Joia, around the block for her morning walk. As I walk my dog and get my steps up, I listen to worship songs that fill my heart with love, faith, and confidence. I'm glad it's early in the morning so that not many people see me because I would be quite a sight. Before I built my relationship with God, I would take Joia out for her walk and jog on the spot every time she stopped to wee, sniff or poop to increase my step count. That was weird enough, and I got plenty of strange looks just doing that. Well, consider what happens now. In addition to jogging on the spot trying to get my steps up, while Joia is doing her thing, I am singing Christian worship songs out aloud, with my hands in the air praising God. Yep, weird! During the day, I commit to reading one chapter in the Bible and, whilst I don't always understand it, I do understand the power of the word of God.

I have always wanted a different life than most. A few years ago, I learned that I need to do things differently from most if I want a different life. If I am doing things differently from most, I know I may look weird, and that's okay. In fact, for me, that is the only way I want it. If I want an exceptional life, and I do, I need to do exceptional things. Prayer, belief in Jesus, and a relationship with God are why I am creating and fulfilling this wonderful life. In my favourite of the Rocky movies, *Rocky Balboa,* Rocky is questioning whether to fight again because of how he may be seen at his age, when his friend Marie says: "It doesn't matter how it looks to other people, it only matters how it looks to you!" Amen.

Now, let's talk 'TEARS of joy' moments that I believe have come from my commitment to my new faith and having the belief and patience to trust God, and know that it will happen, no matter how illogical it may seem. In fact, in his book, **The Force of Faith**, Kenneth Copeland says: *'Faith is not the product of reason'*. He then goes on to say: *'Believers are not led by logic. We are not even to be led by good sense... The world says, seeing is believing. God says, believing is seeing.'* This can be hard to do when the world is pushing for logic and reasoning, but let me tell you, miracles happen when you believe.

Let me start with a small and seemingly trivial one. Before taking Joia out for her morning walk, I can't tell you how many times it is raining. Neither she nor I enjoy the rain. So, I pray to God to hold the rain off for twenty minutes. Now, hear me on this, I have done this at least fifteen times, and every time – yes, I said every time – the rain stops for at least the time we are out walking. That, my friend, is the power of faith.

I had an issue the other day and was having trouble connecting my camera before doing an online training session, so I decided to restart my computer. Then I couldn't get an internet connection. I started to panic because I was thinking logically, not spiritually. So, I restarted the computer again, but I prayed to God to ensure the internet connection and the camera worked. Yep. You guessed it, all spot on. Now, you can argue all you like that it was luck, coincidence, a logical explanation for the camera, the internet, and the rain, but I choose to believe in God. There may not have been 'TEARS of joy' in these situations, but certainly, there was a strong level of peace, confidence, and joy, that's for sure.

What about this one, then? A great friend of mine contacted me to talk. She wasn't sure who else to talk to and shared how she found a lump in her right breast. She had an ultrasound which showed significant growth. As you can imagine, she was concerned, and the darkest thoughts and worst-case scenarios entered her mind. At that moment, I knew logic or advice was not going to be the right course of action, so instead, I handed it over to God. She is also a Christian, so I didn't have to convince her of the next step.

At that moment, we prayed to God for miraculous healing. If you are not a believer in this type of faith, I know how weird this sounds, but believers are not led by logic. They are led by faith. We are led by *believing is seeing*. We prayed, and after we spoke, I rang several other Christians I know and asked them also to pray for my friend. For the next week, I prayed for her every day. One week later, I received this message from her:

> *The initial ultrasound found a large mass. The mammo-gram <u>couldn't find it</u> one week later!*

That, my friend, is what I call a miracle! A miracle that cannot be explained by logic. It was an incredible 'TEARS of joy' moment for my friend. You may think it is just coincidence, luck, or an inaccurate initial ultrasound. However, I choose to believe it was a miracle from God. There is an incredible level of peace that comes with letting go of logic and having faith in a power source outside of your own understanding. For me, over the last few years, it has led to many 'TEARS of joy' moments.

With God's help, many tears have come from finding myself during isolation due to COVID-19. After a character-building journey, tears came when I received a publishing contract for this book. Ark House is a Christian book publisher for which I am incredibly grateful. I believe it is a divine connection from God. My business has expanded through my connections, opportunities to impact lives, wonderful people to collaborate with, and is flowing in a way that only God could orchestrate. I know, hope, and have faith that I am in a loving relationship with my soulmate by the time you are reading this. That will definitely bring me 'TEARS of joy'.

Moving towards 'TEARS of Joy'

Hebrews 11:1 – *Now faith is confidence in what we hope for and assurance about what we do not see.* (NIV)

I could go on and on, but this chapter aims to give you an understanding of who I am at the core and why I am passionate about this message. 'TEARS of joy' moments are available for all of us regularly when we understand where joy comes from. I thought it was material stuff. I was wrong. I thought it was an achievement. I was wrong. I thought it was about my appearance and being admired. Again, I was wrong. It was inside of me the whole time. I just needed to give myself permission to find and experience it.

Without my journey of faith and relationship with God, who forgave me, freed me, and helped me feel like a valuable human being, it would not have happened. At this moment, I want to encourage you to explore a faith position for yourself, whatever that may look like. The 'TEARS of joy' experiences will open for you, as it did for me when you let go of the need to be perfect, forgive yourself of what needs forgiving, build a strong sense of self, and pass your doubts, concerns, and fears to another source.

Key questions and action steps

1. Do you have a nagging feeling that something is missing in your life, but you just can't put your finger on it?
2. If so, the first step is to know, understand, and believe that you don't need to have all the answers. Doesn't that feel great? It sure did for me.
3. Step two is to let go of that need to always be in control, and allow faith to start to seep into your life. That faith may be a

Christian, or some other platform. It could just be having faith in the Universe or something else that you believe in. In my opinion, the bottom line is that without a faith you can trust in, a long life of joy is difficult.

4. With faith, you will see a positive perspective and outcome for every challenge, problem, or adversity in your life. Think about one challenge you have experienced in your life where you learned, grew as a person, or found an opportunity. This will happen every time, with faith.

CHAPTER 4

Start with the end in mind

"Your big picture is critical. It needs to be big, it needs to excite you, it needs to be clear, and it needs to be important enough to move you emotionally."

Aah, that often elusive and misunderstood question. What do you really want? This is the main reason, I believe, there are so many people wandering aimlessly through life just taking what they get. You will remember the famous conversation in *Alice in Wonderland* when Alice asks the Cheshire Cat which direction she should take. The cat says: "That depends on where you want to get to". Alice responds: "It really doesn't matter". The cat says: "Well then, it doesn't really matter which way you go, any path will get you there".

The reality is, everything I will talk about in this book means absolutely nothing if you don't have a clear vision for the type of life you want to live. You may be asking why? Well, it's quite simple. Unless you have a destination in mind, you will be like Alice, and most people, wandering aimlessly through life. It's amazing to me, now that I'm finally enlightened, how so few people take the time to really think about and plan out the amazing life they will be living. I didn't do it for many years of my life and always wondered why I was never happy or fulfilled. It's no surprise. I didn't have the end in mind.

If you were to jump in your car to meet a friend but didn't know the exact location of where the meeting was to take place, how would you go? You would probably drive around for a while until you realised it was a fruitless exercise. It would be unlikely you would randomly bump into them. You would then give up and go home, or you wouldn't even get started in the first place. Isn't it crazy to think you would get in your car and have no idea where you are going? Hmm, that's something to consider as you are driving through your life.

Even setting goals will be frustrating and pointless if you don't have the clarity of a big, colourful, and exciting picture of the life you plan to be living. Each goal you set needs to be a stepping-stone along the path to a bigger and better life, and to fulfilling your purpose, not just a random event. As a personal trainer, I saw so many people set the goal to lose weight for an occasion, such as a wedding or a beach holiday. In most cases, they achieved this finite goal, then got to the other side of that point in time, and put all the weight back on, with interest! Why does that happen so predictably? It's what I've come to know as the *Everest Principle*.

I'm going to explain my understanding of this principle. If it's not totally accurate, don't worry, the message is what I want you to embed in your thinking. I only wish I knew about it earlier in my life. It refers to the many people who have attempted to climb the awe-inspiring Mt Everest. Apparently many people who lost their lives in climbing Mt Everest died, after successfully reaching the summit, and were on their way back down.

Can you imagine it? These champions had undertaken all the work, all the preparation, and all the sacrifice. They experienced all the pain and discomfort to get to the top of the highest mountain in the world. Then, as they relaxed, celebrated, and headed down the mountain to enjoy their massive achievement, they died. Why? The *Everest Principle*! They had only set the goal to reach the top of the mountain. They didn't set the goal to get back to the bottom.

They lost their edge and stopped doing the things they had done to get to the top. They got complacent. They got lazy. They thought getting to the bottom would just be an easy journey. Just as they thought it would be okay and they were winners, the conditions changed, they were unprepared, and they paid the ultimate price for complacency.

Call it the *Everest Principle*, call it a big picture, call it a mission, call it a purpose, call it the goal-beyond-the-goal, call it whatever you like. Any and every goal can only be successful long-term if it's a stepping-stone in the journey of reaching and achieving a much bigger vision or purpose. That doesn't mean you are never satisfied with where you are at in life, or are always wanting more. In fact, it means the opposite. You may have heard the saying, *success is not a destination, success is a journey*. If you have, and you genuinely believe it, then it is an exciting time. You are in the present, working towards a better future, which gives life excitement, optimism, and fulfilment.

I didn't always believe *success is a journey*. I always believed success was measured by the destination, the win, and the achievement of a goal. When I was an aspiring athlete, working to become a professional footballer, the journey was frustrating, painful, discouraging, gut-wrenching and, at times, heartbreaking. I just wanted it over and to be running through the banner as a senior footballer. Looking back now, however, the things I talk about regularly and those I am most proud of are the things I went through and overcame to achieve the goal. It was the journey. When I decided to write my first book, I was working over 100 hours per week. It was inconvenient and uncomfortable, and it seemed to take forever to get it written. At the time, all I wanted was the achievement and holding the published book in my hands. Guess what I treasure, talk about, and teach most now? Yep, the journey.

Even today, I aspire to write more books, speak on more stages, impact more lives, and build my influence to fulfil the purpose God has created me for. I am learning to become far more aware of the power and joy found in each moment, even the frustrating and discouraging ones. Everything that happens in my life, each day, seemingly good or bad, I celebrate. It sounds weird, but I have faith that great things are divinely created. The challenges are also a gift from God to help me be better, get stronger, learn more and/or open doors of opportunity for me to walk through.

Anyway, I digressed on a little detour. Sorry, I'm back now. The point is your big picture is critical. It doesn't necessarily need to be big and scary. It does need to excite you, it needs to be clear, and it needs to be important enough to move you emotionally. I was sitting in a seminar several years ago, and the guy speaking talked about how he was struggling to achieve things in his life. He was suffering from anxiety, stress, procrastination, and lethargy. He explained how one day he started to think about what an ideal day would look like for him if time and money were of no consequence. He spent an hour or so detailing this ideal day, from the moment he got up to the moment he went to bed. When he'd done it, he was excited. From that moment, every decision he had to make was easier because it had to contribute to fulfilling this ideal day.

With that in mind, I got to work on my own ideal day, and this is what I came up with:

> *I am financially free because I add incredible value to the world.*

> *I wake up early and bounce of bed with passion and purpose, excited about a new day. My bedroom overlooks an amazing water vista in one of my homes in Australia, the USA or Hungary.*

I get up, do some exercise, have a healthy breakfast, and go for a walk along the waterfront with my soulmate, and my dog. I thank God for my abundant life.

I then settle into my office (with the inspiring view) for a couple of hours to write my next best-selling book, create a program, and record a podcast.

I speak to more than 1,000 teenagers and/or adults at a seminar, workshop, or conference, and share my message to inspire them to live a purposeful life of joyful longevity. It is my mission and purpose to create a wave of well-being all around the world.

In the evening, I spend time with the people I care about the most. My personal chef has cooked an incredible meal. The long table on the balcony, overlooking the brilliant vista, is covered with a delicious spread of beautiful fresh food and drink.

We eat, drink, laugh, share, and are merry! I go to bed full… full of great food, full of joy, full of love, and full of life! I thank God for my abundant life.

An ideal day!

What a difference this one exercise has made in my life. I've printed it off, added images, and it sits on the wall in my office. In fact, I'm looking at it right now. I look at it and imagine it several times every day. This vision energises me and fuels my purpose and drives my actions every day. I can see the inspiring view from my balconies. I can see my new books on the store bookshelves. I can visualise looking out over an audience of thousands as I get up to speak. I can feel the warm breeze on my face. I can feel the soft hand of the person I love in mine as we walk along the waterfront. I can smell the beautifully fresh and tasty food. I can feel the immense joy and satisfaction of my achievements. I am energised and excited as I know it will be done.

In fact, this same vision inspired a month-long trip to the USA in September 2019 to launch my book, *The Wellness Puzzle,* and start this wave of wellness. It was a trip that brought the vision to life and fuelled the passion and determination to make it happen. It turned those things I imagined into reality. The inspiring views, the great people, the amazing contacts and collaborations, the audiences, the impact, and the amazing smells and tastes of this big, beautiful world. It was a wonderful trip in pursuit of my dream.

Again, I want to emphasise I don't spend my life, nor do I recommend you spend yours, living in the future. I have the vision because it gives my day today more meaning and passion. There is something exciting about waking up every day and looking forward to what it will bring. Each moment is an adventure and one that will present your pieces of the puzzle to help you put together your wonderful vision. As I'm sure you know, the most important thing about successfully completing a puzzle is the picture on the front of the box. Imagine 1,000 pieces of a jigsaw puzzle with no picture? How long would it be before those pieces were carefully filed under *R* for rubbish in the trash can? Unlike a jigsaw puzzle where there is a picture on the front of the box, you will need to come up with your own picture representing success and fulfilment in your life.

It can be easy to lose sight of your ideal day if you are distracted by the busyness of your life and the noise of the world around you. It is so critical to stay emotionally connected to your vision. I wrote the description of my ideal day a few years ago. When I wrote it, typed it, found pictures to bring it to life and stuck it all around the house, I was excited, focused and determined. I got into action doing what I needed to do, but over time was distracted by the many things I was trying to focus on each day.

I was thinking about it less and less frequently each day. As the days, weeks and months went by, I was looking but not really seeing the images and descriptions on the wall. Although I was still talking about it, I'm not sure if my faith was there, or that my belief was strong. So, I wasn't really moving in that direction. In 2018, I talked to a gentleman I just met, now a great friend, and told him about this vision of mine. I think he must have seen in my eyes I was just talking the talk but not really walking the walk.

Now, keep in mind this was a man I had only just met. I had just finished talking about my plans to be living, loving, writing, and inspiring in the USA and around the world. He looked at me and asked: "So Andrew, why aren't you already doing it?" Wow, talk about a show-stopper! I certainly wasn't expecting that question from a man I had just met for the first time. I stumbled and fumbled for an answer and then paused and just said: "Good question". I pretended in front of him I was cool, but deep down, I was angry. Maybe initially angry with him for being so direct, but really, I was angry with myself for letting this dream and vision slide out of my determined focus. The good news, from that moment, it was back and stronger than before. I came home and had a serious conference with myself. Through collaboration with an amazing lady in St Louis, USA, I arranged the one-month trip to the USA in September 2019. This trip, as I mentioned, re-energised and re-focused me, and I am more determined than ever to make this dream a 'TEARS-of-joy' reality.

Author **JK Rowling** is living a life beyond anything she could have imagined when she had the idea to write *Harry Potter and the Philosopher's Stone*. She was a single mother, living on welfare, suffering depression, and even considered suicide. She decided to take the one skill she had and turn it into something. When she wrote the first book in the Harry Potter series, she knew she had more than a book. However, I don't think she could ever have predicted the *Harry Potter Franchise* would be worth more than 25 billion dollars.

She had a vision of a better life for her and her daughter. She was clear about the type of life she wanted to live, the difference she wanted to make, the places she wanted to travel, and the people she wanted to meet. She developed a clear and powerful vision that was the catalyst for her astronomical success. Suppose her goal was just to have a book published, with no bigger vision. Do you honestly believe she would have had the resilience, courage, and persistence to overcome forty publisher rejections? I'm pretty sure there were 'TEARS of joy' when it finally happened.

In 1952, **Colonel Harland Sanders**, at age 62, started Kentucky Fried Chicken (KFC). I wonder whether he would have imagined the global phenomenon KFC would become many decades later. When he was broke, he survived on a paltry pension and lived in his van. His only skill was the ability to cook. His only possession, of any value, was a recipe for southern fried chicken. I wonder what his vision really was. If he were alive today, I would love to ask him. I think if it were just to make enough money to buy his next meal, we would not know KFC today in the 21st century.

You see, there had to be a bigger vision and a burning desire for Colonel Sanders to overcome what he had to face in the process of selling his recipe. I talk about this man often, not because I think you should rush out and buy KFC food, but because he is an inspiring example of the strength of a clear and powerful vision. According to my sources, when he was almost on the verge of giving up on life, he sat under a tree writing his suicide letter. Suddenly, for some reason, he started writing what he would have accomplished if he had his life over again. He realised there was so much he hadn't done yet. The one thing he knew he could do better than everyone else was cooking. And so was born one last idea. He knew he had a great recipe, and he knew that someone would pay for it. His idea was to go to restaurants, give them his recipe, and receive a percentage of any sales in return.

It sounded like a good idea to him, so he started with enthusiasm, his eyes and heart firmly fixed on his new vision. What he wasn't expecting was the amount of rejection he would face. But his dream, his vision, and the strong emotional connection to it kept him going until he finally found one restaurant owner who said yes. KFC was born. That one <u>yes</u> came after 1009 rejections! That is the power of a clear and emotionally compelling vision.

Moving towards 'TEARS of Joy'

> Proverbs 29:18 – *Where there is no vision, the people perish: but he that keepeth the law, happy is he.* (KJV)

I think I have made my point loud and clear in this chapter. However, just in case you are an ex-footballer like me who has been knocked around the head too many times, I will reinforce it right now. I have introduced a formula that will generate a predictable outcome to create 'TEARS of joy' in your life so that you continue to enjoy happiness, well-being, and abundance. However, the glue to make this formula work depends on a clear and powerful vision for the life you want to live. What is the picture on the front of your life puzzle box? What is the ideal day when you will know you have done what's required and followed through on a wonderful journey?

I can tell you the hardest work is done when you have worked this out. This is when you are clear about your vision and the life you want, and are powerfully and emotionally connected to it. If you skip this part and think you don't need to do it, you will probably end up frustrated, discouraged, and stuck. Please don't be like me. I thought I would just keep doing it my way, just to prove to myself it was wrong, time and time again. I have set so many goals that I didn't achieve because of the *Everest Principle*. I refused to visualise and design my ideal day because I didn't understand each goal was a stepping-stone to achieving my passionate pursuit.

Unless you take this first step, the rest of what I will talk about in this book, while possibly interesting and hopefully entertaining, will be fruitless for you. It's your life. Please don't let it pass you by because you refuse to invest a small amount of time planning what it will be like when you are doing the things you are passionate about. The following steps are what I suggest you do from here. I hope you will take my advice and action them.

Key questions and action steps

1. Can you find thirty minutes in your hectic schedule to sit quietly, with no distractions? If you can, think about what is most important to you, what you want to achieve, and how you want your life to look.

2. Assuming you answered yes, get yourself some paper or a notebook. Now imagine a scenario when you have all the time and money you need, you are on purpose, with the people you care about, and you are optimally healthy. If you have no restrictions, what would your ideal day look like? Where would you live? Who would you be with? What would you be doing? Where would you be travelling? Who will be impacted? Create a clear and exciting written description of this ideal day.

3. Now, take that description, type or write it on paper and stick it on your wall(s). Add images and quotes that give meaning

and create a powerful emotional response every time you look at them, and read them.

4. Look at it and imagine it every single day. Experience the sights, the scenes, the smells, and the feelings that go with living that day.

5. Take it for a test drive, whenever you can, just like my one-month trip to the USA.

6. Keep adding to this visual and keep it in the front of your mind.

7. This is your true north. This is the magnet that will pull you, lead you and inspire you to follow the 'TEARS of joy' process and use it to create this day and the 'TEARS of joy' you will experience.

CHAPTER 5

Purpose gives vision power

"From my personal experience, I have discovered a vision is a picture of the life you want to live, a purpose is your underlying meaning for that life."

As I talked about in the last chapter, the vision I have had for much of my life has become clearer and stronger over the last few years. Now, without wanting to sound like I contradict what I explained in the last chapter, let me just say this. A clear vision is important, but without the power of purpose, I'm not sure it holds enough strength to move you through the process of change to significant 'TEARS of joy' moments. You may be asking: *So what's the difference?* This is an awesome question and one I will answer from my perspective in this chapter.

In my book, *The Wellness Puzzle*, I discuss seven puzzle pieces that help people create optimal wellbeing and live their best life. The first and, in my opinion, the most important piece of the puzzle is finding purpose. I truly believe once you find your purpose, as a power source to your vision, the rest seems to take care of itself. In other words, the fire-in-the-belly is strong, the determination becomes natural, resilience is automatic, and persistence will be your greatest weapon. Well, it is certainly the case for me. So, let's explore the difference between a vision and your purpose. It's a critical distinction to make and understand if an ongoing stream of 'TEARS of joy' moments sounds good to you.

I am about to give you my interpretation of the difference. It may not be yours, and it may vary from what other people may believe or have said. From my personal experience, I have discovered a vision is a picture of the life you want to live, a purpose is your underlying meaning for that life. The vision is the destination. The purpose is the fuel to get you there and help you overcome the obstacles and challenges that will come your way on the journey.

One of my favourite movies is *City Slickers*. The movie is about Mitch Robbins, who just turned 39 years old, married with two children, and lost his way. He is not clear on his purpose. His two best friends buy him a two-week holiday driving cattle across the American Midwest. On the cattle drive, he gets to know the leader, a true cowboy named Curly. When Curly talks about his passion for bringing in a herd, Mitch can see that Curly has found his purpose. The following conversation is what helps Mitch on his own journey.

> **Curly**: *You city folk worry about a lotta shit, don't ya?*

> **Mitch**: *Shit? My wife basically told me she doesn't want me around.*

> **Curly**: *How old are you? 38?*

> **Mitch**: *I'm 39.*

> **Curly**: *Yeah, you all come up about the same age, with the same problems. You spend fifty weeks getting knots in*

your rope and then you think two weeks up here will untie them for you. None of you get it...

Curly: *Do you know what the secret of life is?*

Mitch: *No, what?*

Curly: *This (he holds up one finger).*

Mitch: *Your finger?*

Curly: *One thing. Just one thing. You stick to that, and everything else don't mean shit.*

Mitch: *That's great but, what's the one thing?*

Curly: *That's what you've got to figure out.*

It is a great movie and very much worth watching. It's amazing when you want to watch a light-hearted and entertaining movie, and you get some profound stuff when you least expect it. Who knew cowboy Curly would offer the secret to purpose in such a simple but powerful way? The bottom line is you are on this planet for a purpose. You are not a mistake. There is no way you could accidentally be here. The odds against your existence are far too great. I am a true believer in Creation, not Evolution. In my mind, Evolution, as a biological process, leaves out the miracle and purpose theory, which I wholeheartedly believe in.

Purpose, however, is one of those ethereal concepts that can be hard to get your head around and put your finger on. There is no doubt, it can be difficult to define your own purpose. However, if I could suggest you start with the knowledge and belief, you have one. Otherwise, God would not have breathed life into you. As Curly said to Mitch, it is *one thing*, but what that thing is, and how we find it, is the challenge. This chapter aims to help you start the process and explore the idea you have a purpose, and the odds are your purpose has a face.

By the way, Mitch did discover his *one thing* on that cattle drive, and it had a face. In fact, they were the faces of his wife and two children. To make identifying your purpose easier, why not go with the idea that purpose has a face! What do I mean? I think the best way to explain this critical concept is with some real-life examples. Let's start with an Austrian Psychologist, Viktor Frankl, who wrote a book you have possibly heard of called *Man's Search for Meaning*. In the 1940s, Viktor and his new bride were captured by the Nazis, separated, and incarcerated in concentration camps. In his book, Viktor journals his horrific experiences over four years of brutality, frostbite, abuse, starvation, and violence.

He watched men around him giving up all hope of life and dying. He searched for meaning to help him survive and thrive through the inhuman conditions. He knew one thing that gave this journey meaning, was the deep love he had for his wife. When he envisioned her face, the brutality seemed bearable, the starvation seemed tolerable, and the frostbite seemed sufferable. He knew he needed to get through one day at a time and, each minute of each day, his focus was on the face, that he adored, and the lady he would do anything be with again.

Even though Viktor never saw his wife again, his love for her gave the experience meaning. He used it to learn, grow, and later impact millions of lives. For many decades, people have been guided by him to find their meaning, identify the face or faces that give their life purpose. Viktor did this through his psychological counselling and his book, long after being liberated from his four-year incarceration. As he settled back into his psychology practice after the war, he would use his experience to help others in an incredibly unique way. When dealing with depressed and even suicidal people, he would ask them in a compassionate way why they hadn't followed through and taken their own lives. In every case, these troubled people would mention their love and/or responsibility for another person, or people, as the reason for not taking their life. Hmm, that is something to consider.

In the early stages of this book, I mentioned my mother for a good reason. She is a shining and inspiring example of the power of the message of this chapter and book. In her case and in my mind, how she outlived a terminal cancer diagnosis by fifteen years comes down to one thing, and one thing only. After the secondary cancer diagnosis and the pessimistic prognosis, she stopped, reflected, found, and tapped into the power source that was her purpose. And yes, it had faces. It was her family who gave her life meaning – her husband, children, and grandchildren.

Wow! From that moment, to watch her embrace the change required to allow an additional fifteen years, the medical profession didn't predict, or expect, inspires me every day. My mother passed away in 2004. Her memory and legacy live on in my heart, thoughts, words, and actions. It is the reason I wrote *Dance Until it Rains*. It is the reason why I spend so much time helping people live their best life. It is the reason why my message about purpose is so passionate and strong. The faces of her family were her powerful purpose. I believe this was why she fulfilled so many things she visualised and helped her experience many 'TEARS of joy' moments.

As I mentioned earlier, for much of my life I have chased things that I thought were purposeful. I thought my purpose was connected to my fame as a professional footballer, it wasn't. I believed my purpose was connected to the admiration I got because of my physique. I was wrong again. I even believed becoming an author and being known and respected was where my purpose lay. Even there, I was incorrect. The moment of realisation came to me about six months after my first book was published.

At the time, I was just chuffed with myself for becoming an author, something I never thought I would or could do. My ego was being fed, but something intangible was still missing. The same thing had been missing my entire life, until one moment on one particular day. Up until then, being an author was a cool thing. It was good for my ego and a great way to improve my credibility. That was until I received an email that included, *'your book has had a profound effect on my life'*, and *'it has changed my life'*, and *'I push your book to everyone who asks how I did it. Thank you'*.

I finished reading this email and wiped away the 'TEARS of joy', satisfaction, and fulfilment from my eyes. I was hooked. I knew my purpose. It was that fast. The credibility, recognition, and money I made were not even close to the joy I felt reading the email, knowing the impact I made on and in that man's life. A man, by the way, I had never met or will probably never meet. The feeling welled up inside me that I had the power to impact lives and make a difference. Every day since that moment in 2004, I have bounced out of bed full of joy, full of anticipation, and full of purpose to make the day count and impact more lives. It was always about other people. My purpose has faces, many, many faces.

Deborah Stathis is the author of a book called *Beyond Trauma*. At the age of 19, she lost control of her 1985 Toyota Corolla, with no air-bags, on a slippery road, and wrapped her car around a telegraph pole. The result was devastating. Her face was a mess, her brain was damaged, and doctors were telling her that life would never be the same, and she would have to get used to never living life as she had planned. Deb is one of the greatest inspirations in my life. When she looked at her broken face, sunken cheek, non-functioning eye, half-shaven head, a scar from ear-to-ear across her skull, she asked herself: *'So, what are you going to do now? Are you going to accept this or live a life of meaning, significance, and joy? It's your choice.'*

I think it's obvious the choice she made. Let me tell you, the path was tough and fraught with pain, discomfort, doubt, fear, and discouragement. Today, more than twenty years later, despite the trauma she experiences every day since her accident, she is living an exceptional life and positively impacting many people. Looking at her, you would never know what she has been through. Talking to her you will find a lady full of passion, purpose, and the joys of life. What was it that got her through the pain, suffering, and ongoing trauma to be where she is today? It was faces. Most obviously, her own face she wanted to get back to the way it was. It was the faces of the people she cared about; her parents, her family, her friends, and the lives she could influence.

This final and powerful story is about Kate, a great friend of mine. She had an incredibly traumatic childhood of abuse, which destroyed trust, her self-esteem, and led her down a very unsavoury path. Things were so bad she was on track for total self-destruction at a young age if her purpose didn't appear. I have enormous respect for Kate's courage as she has allowed me to share part of her story in this book.

The result of being sexually and emotionally violated over many years as a child was that her innocence, trust, and feelings of security were ripped away. The incredible loneliness she felt came from not having a protector or anyone she could go to for help to stop the ongoing violation. However, she did have a strong circle of friends at school who helped her feel some level of safety and security.

Kate needed a way to run from her pain and initially found alcohol. She and some of her friends started drinking at age twelve. She explained she was drinking purely to get drunk and escape from the pain she felt. In fact, they would steal whatever alcohol they could from their own homes and pour it into one container and drink the concoction, no matter how it tasted. This went on for three to four years and was escalating. As they were on the verge of taking their addictive behaviour to the next level, there was divine intervention.

Kate and her friends had arranged to buy some heavy drugs they were planning to start taking. In fact, they ordered these drugs from a dealer and were waiting for the delivery. Before the drugs were delivered, Kate and her friends decided to attend a Christian camp. They saw the camp as a way to get away from home, sneak off to the nearby town, and get into mischief. Thankfully, something happened at this camp that helped Kate find her purpose and change the direction of her life.

The change started happening in Kate's heart during the morning worship, where they would listen to and sing along with Christian songs and play games. A verse mentioned in one of the songs was from Isaiah 41:10, which said: *'Fear not, for I am with you'.* This verse had a profound impact on Kate as she had always felt abandoned and alone.

Then, one morning the youth leader spoke about how Jesus died on the cross for all our sins, and we are all worthy of Him dying for us. At that moment, it hit Kate. She felt and believed she was worthy of God's love, and for Jesus to die for her. The feeling hit her so strongly, and she became so overwhelmed with emotion, she had to get out of the room. She ran out of the meeting, hid behind a bin, and started sobbing. She was releasing the build-up of many years of trauma, pain, hurt, and emotion.

She was found by one of the youth pastors, who sat down and prayed for her. Right then, she gave her life to Christ, and everything changed for her. She saw overwhelming love. She saw the face of Christ. For the first time, she was not alone in the world. She explained to me how no one understood how alone she was at the time. Then, in a heartbeat, the whole world looked different, her fear was gone, and it was replaced with love. She has since raised two beautiful daughters. Her role as a personal trainer has a powerful impact on many people's lives. With God's purpose in her heart, she is sharing her story to help the many victims of abuse. Her purpose has a face – the face of Jesus Christ.

To finish this story of the incredible Kate, she has given me permission to share an entry she recently wrote in her journal. It took courage to write this, and even more to allow me to include it in this book for the world to read. This is powerful, so I think you may need to be seated.

The thief comes only to steal, kill, and destroy. I have come that they may have life and have it to the full. John 10:10

You were fed lies when you were a child. You were held down and robbed of your innocence. You were not to blame for the cruel and evil attacks. Your little body was not meant to hold this much pain. You, as a child, should never have had to experience fear in the most horrible way – it was never God's plan for you.

You grew without love and protection, and yet light shined in the darkness, somehow always for you. That one cry out from a little girl who did not know God Almighty, was heard by Him. It was always God's Light with the child, with the teenager and young woman. He gently whispered: *'Fear not, for I am with you'.*

Be strong and courageous. Do not be afraid, do not be discouraged, for the Lord your God will be with you wherever you go. Joshua 1:9.

Whether you are a believer or not, I want you to try and imagine what Kate experienced at the youth camp. She went from a childhood of abuse and sexual violation, feeling worthless and unloved, to being supported, loved, and protected by God. You can argue as much as you like that God doesn't exist, but you can't argue with the transformation that happened in Kate's heart and life at the youth camp.

Make no mistake about it. You are here for a reason, you have a purpose, and that purpose has a face or many faces.

Moving towards 'TEARS of Joy'

> Proverbs 20:5 – *The purposes of a person's heart are deep waters, but one who has insight draws them out.* (NIV)

As I unpack the 'TEARS of joy' formula in the next few chapters, it is vital you know and understand the importance of what I have covered so far. Without these strong foundational layers for the 'TEARS of joy' formula to stand on, it will collapse like a house built on a swamp. It doesn't matter how well a house is built, if there is no foundation, it will not stand. You must have a clear vision, there definitely needs to be a strong desire but, more than anything, there needs to be meaning and purpose for everything you strive for. It will keep you standing and strong when things look bleak, when negative opinions weigh you down and when doubt starts to set in.

What else would keep Nelson Mandela enduring 27 years of incarceration if not for a powerful purpose which had many faces attached to it? He said: "What counts in life is not the mere fact that we have lived. It is what difference we have made to the lives of others that will determine the significance of the life we lead." What else would keep Mother Teresa thriving in a life of poverty if not for the desire to make a difference in the life of many people? She said: "Spread love everywhere you go. Let no one ever come to you without leaving happier." What else would keep Fred Hollows travelling to third-world countries, and treating the eyesight of people, if not for the smiles he bought to the faces of the many people he treated? He said: "To my mind, having a care and concern for others is the highest of the human qualities".

As you get yourself ready for the rest and the best of your life, spend some time to get clear on the person you want to become, and the life you want to live. Then find the purpose – that you absolutely have – to give that vision the fuel and power to fly. The mistake many make is waiting for tragedy or adversity to strike before really zoning in on their purpose. Can I suggest you start the process now, while you have the choice and life is great? I promise you, it will add an incredible element of joy, it will give your life direction, and it will give you the meaning that will fuel everything you do.

Key questions and action steps

1. When you wake up each morning, are you excited for a new day or feel anxious and uncertain?
2. The above question will help you identify if you have a purpose. Please, if the answer is the latter, pay attention to the next few questions, ideas, and action steps.
3. Do you believe you are on this planet for a purpose? If not, can I suggest you start to work out the odds of your physical existence, as it may help you realise your being alive is no accident?
4. Identifying purpose can be challenging. Whether you are a believer or not, why not start with a prayer to God and ask for a sign.
5. Who are the faces you would do anything for, and give your life meaning? It may well be your own face.
6. Do you feel like the life you have lived, the things you have experienced, and the lessons you have learned on your journey could help other people in their lives?

7. If anything was possible, what impact would you want to have, and what legacy would you want to leave on this world?

8. How would it feel if you were able to make a positive difference in the lives of others?

9. Can I suggest you spend some time thinking about your strengths, interests, and experiences, and how you can take them and use them to help other people? This, my friend, is the beginning of finding purpose.

CHAPTER 6

Everything starts with a thought

"It was not that I categorically believed I could do it. I just didn't know that I couldn't."

I t's easy to blame situations, circumstances and other people for the results and outcomes we experience in life. No one is immune to the strong emotional pull towards victim thinking and blame. What happened to me many years ago is a good example. I had given my professional football club seven years of my life, and much of my blood, sweat and tears. Imagine my astonishment when I read that I had been de-listed in a national newspaper.

That's a polite and publicly humiliating way of saying I was sacked, dumped, and discarded. It was just two weeks after the end of the 1987 season, and I had played what I thought was a good game in the reserve-grade grand final for the club. To say I was shocked would be the understatement of the year.

I sat there numb for a little while, trying to comprehend what I had just read before I launched into an almighty earth-shattering tantrum!

I went into poor-little-ole-me victim mode and scathingly blamed everything and everyone I could. Everyone except me, of course. I blamed the club, the coaches, the fans, and even the other players. I blamed my lack of ability, my skinny frame, and my bad luck. I blamed everything and everyone except the one thing that was indeed to blame. It was me and my thoughts!

You see, if I am honest, the downward slide leading to my inevitable and seemingly surprising catastrophe all started about a year earlier. I am going to be transparent and vulnerable right now and possibly seriously incriminate myself. Why? There are two reasons. I want to show you the devastating impact of wrong thoughts. I also want to help you identify any potential wrong thinking in yourself and stop it before it is too late. Is that okay? I want to start the story a little earlier, so you can see the amazing power of thoughts. They will raise you to an astonishing and unlikely 'TEARS of joy' type success or drag you down to agonising *tears of pain* type regret.

I have mentioned in previous books and blogs I am a middle child. I was quite insecure and was always an attention seeker. As a younger child and teen, I was quite skinny, often sick, and very much a mama's boy. One of the first toys I got was an iron and ironing board, so I could do the ironing next to my mother. All I can say, in my own defence, is… mama's boy! When I was around twelve, I had a thought. Not a sensible or logical thought but, at the time, a good thought, nevertheless. I decided to be a professional Australian Rules footballer because I wanted attention, admiration, and validation. The fact that I was skinny, sickly, and not that talented didn't seem to dissuade me. I had the thought, got excited, made the decision and off I went.

That simple thought started the 'TEARS of joy' process. Somehow, with vision, focus, work, desire, and creating the right routines, at the age of sixteen I was invited to participate in pre-season training at the St Kilda Football Club, a professional club in Melbourne, Australia. I will talk more about the journey, and its ups and downs, at different stages of this book. After a couple of years of hard work, determination, and persistence, I became a regular senior player, and my dream was realised. But then, about a year or so before the fateful sacking, my thoughts changed.

As embarrassing as it is to admit it, the main reason I wanted to be a professional footballer was to feel valued, accepted and admired. Little did I know, at that time of my life, those feelings could never come from any external source or achievement. They had to come from inside me. As I mentioned earlier, I was continually chasing something I could never reach. With hard work and persistence, I made it to the senior team and was a regular senior footballer. As confusing as it was at the time, I didn't feel any better about myself. Sure, my ego was being fed, but not my soul or my self-esteem.

At the time, despite not feeling the way I hoped I would, I thought I had made it as a successful footballer. I thought I didn't need to work as hard. I thought about how sick of the pain, discomfort and suffering to get to the top I was, and that my previous few years of effort and achievement were enough to keep me there. I'm sure you can imagine the emotions, actions, and routines initiated from these debilitating thoughts. Training became a chore instead of an opportunity, and stressful instead of empowering. My focus was more easily distracted. My efforts were not as intense or sustained, my habits not as consistent, and my performance was dropping. Consequently, the inevitable happened on that fateful Saturday morning, two weeks after the 1987 Grand Final.

After reading the newspaper in the morning, I was not in the logical or rational state to understand the cause-and-effect reality leading to that moment. I didn't want to know or believe it was my fault. I refused to take any responsibility and launched into a victim-minded, blame-shifting, and scathing attack on anyone or anything I could pass responsibility to. These thoughts I had, because of this event, kept me spiralling. Why? Because the negative thoughts led to negative emotions, which moved me to do things that today I regret and even cringe at.

I went to the club with fire in my eyes. I sat in front of the coach and let him have it! I said things I'm not proud of, I said things that ruined any possibility of another chance, and I said things I have regretted ever since. I held on to the resentment and bitterness towards the club for many years, and I ruined any chance of continuing a professional career. It all started with the thoughts, *it's not fair, why me, it's not my fault.* These are dangerous thoughts because the flow-on effect will bring tears, not 'TEARS of joy', but *tears of pain* and regret. I can tell you, more than three decades after that event, I still have occasional dreams while I sleep about being a successful football player. So, the regret is still there.

While I don't want to dwell on negatives, rather what is possible in your life, you must understand the devastating long-term impact of focusing on the wrong thoughts. I want you to have no doubt that every outcome, good or bad, results from the thoughts you choose to keep or change. Yes, the thoughts you choose to keep or change. We get to control the thoughts, beliefs, and perspectives we hold on to and focus on.

There is powerful evidence of this when we look at successful people, like JK Rowling, who came from less-than-ideal circumstances. We compare two people with the same circumstances, getting totally different outcomes in life. It can only come down to the thoughts they choose to focus on. The next chapter will provide strategies to help identify and re-program limiting and destructive thought patterns.

The website www.protomag.com features an article called, '*Same Genes, Different Fates*', and it starts:

EPPIE LEDERER AND PAULINE PHILLIPS was one of the most famous pairs of identical twins in the United States during the 20th century. Born seventeen minutes apart, both women became wildly popular syndicated columnists – as Ann Landers and Abigail Van Buren, respectively – and dispensed tart-tongued advice about love and other matters. Photos from their younger days reveal that the two women were uncanny look-alikes, both graced with fashion-model cheekbones and vibrant eyes.

Over the years, ever-changing hairstyles made it easier to tell them apart. But it was their dramatically diverging health, finally, that truly distinguished one from the other. Eppie died of multiple myeloma at age 83, while Pauline lived to be 94 before succumbing to Alzheimer's disease this year. That may seem surprising – after all, as identical twins, they have perfectly matched DNA.

The article, amongst other things, then goes on to say:

A large-scale study of identical twins may help elucidate some ways that environment and lifestyle choices alter epigenetics. Launched in 2010, EpiTwin was founded by epigenetic epidemiologist Tim Spector of King's College in London and included about 5,000 identical twins. Every three years, each twin's blood is analysed for possible changes in methylation patterns at 20 million sites in the DNA. "People called us mad when we started collecting DNA more than once, because the prevailing wisdom was that it couldn't change," says Spector, author of *Identically Different: Why You Can Change Your Genes*. Yet he and his colleagues have indeed found alterations in participants' methylation patterns.

This article talks about health and longevity. One of the main determining factors of the health of DNA and living longer is environment and lifestyle. Guess how we end up in and are impacted by a certain environment? Guess how we develop lifestyle habits? It is our thoughts and emotions, choices, actions, and habits that result. Now wellbeing is just one of the different ways we can see differences between twins or other people with the same circumstances. What about people who come from quite different backgrounds, varying circumstances and create results that seem surprising and very unlikely? How can that be explained?

I was listening to Simon Sinek deliver a TED talk, and he spoke about three people who wonderfully demonstrate the power of thoughts. We have heard of **Orville and Wilbur Wright**, but most people don't know **Samuel Pierpont Langley.** Back in the early 20th century, the pursuit of powered flight was all the rage, and many people were trying it. Langley was an astronomer, physicist, aviation pioneer, and inventor of the bolometer. The bolometer measures the power of incident electromagnetic radiation via heating a material with a temperature-dependent electrical resistance. Most people would consider this to be a recipe for success. Not only that, but Langley was also given $50,000 by the War Department to figure out the flying machine, so money was no problem. He held a seat at Harvard, worked at the Smithsonian, and was extremely well-connected with all the educated and intellectuals of the time. He hired the best minds money could find, and the market conditions were fantastic. The New York Times followed Langley around, and everyone was rooting for him. That being the case, why is it very few people have ever heard of Samuel Pierpont Langley?

At about the same time in history, Orville and Wilbur Wright were also attempting man-powered flight. They had none of what we consider to be the elements for success. They had no money and so paid for their dream with the proceeds from their bicycle shop. Not a single person on the Wright brothers' team had a college education, not even Orville or Wilbur. The New York Times didn't even know who they were.

The difference was that Orville and Wilbur were driven by their thinking. They had a cause, a purpose, and a belief. They believed if they could figure out this flying machine, it would change the course of the world. On the other hand, Langley wanted to be rich and famous. He was pursuing the result and the riches. When things got tough for him, he started to question what he was doing, doubting himself and justifying why it would be okay if he never achieved it. In contrast, the Wright brothers had a strong vision, a burning desire, and a solution-oriented mindset. Every time the Wright brothers went out, they would have to take five sets of parts because that's how many times they would crash before supper.

Eventually, on 17 December 1903, the Wright brothers took flight, and no one was there to experience it. The world found out about it a few days later. Further proof Langley suffered from the wrong thinking was on the day he discovered the Wright brothers took flight. It was the day he quit. He could have said: "That's an amazing discovery, guys, and I will improve upon your technology", but he didn't. Langley wasn't the first. He didn't get rich. He didn't get famous, so he quit. The main difference between the Wright brothers and Langley was not their background, education, connections, money, or potential, even though there were significant differences in Langley's favour. The critical difference was the thoughts that dominated their minds.

As I think back over my journey, I was around twelve years old when the thought entered my mind to be a professional footballer. Where it came from. I'm not sure. Why I thought it was a logical idea, again, I'm not sure. How I was going to get there, I had no clue. But none of that mattered because, in my naïve and innocent mind, the decision had been made. I visualised it, I dreamed about it, I talked about it incessantly, and I simply knew it would happen. For me, the most important thought in the process was <u>not</u> that I categorically believed I could do it. I just didn't know that I couldn't.

This is what I believe stops most people from getting started and following through to achieve a goal or aspiration. In their minds, and with their perspective, they come to the erroneous and unsubstantiated conclusion they can't do it. Why erroneous? Simple, they have no proof or conclusive evidence to categorically confirm they can't do it. It's all stories and lies we make up in our own heads. Can you see how critically important your thoughts are?

So, in my young, naïve, and believing mind, I simply decided to give it a go, with my eyes firmly fixed on a successful outcome. Now, at that time, I had no idea of what would be required or how long it would take, but I was not going to be denied. When I was invited to train at St Kilda at the age of sixteen, my world, body and mind were about to be radically stretched, tested, and expanded. I had dreamed about the success, the glamour, the fame, but not for one moment did I consider the price I would have to pay to achieve it.

Fifteen minutes into my very first training session at the club, I realised it would be no *walk in the park*. It was a beautiful Saturday morning in September 1980. The entire under 19s squad met at the beach for what I thought would be a pleasant introductory 10 km (6 mile) run. I expected we would just be cruising along the picturesque track at the top of the cliff, enjoying the beautiful coastal scenery. Boy, did I get it wrong? There are many words I could use to describe that session. *Cruising* is not one of them.

We started running at a disturbingly fast pace, and not too far along the track, we took a detour that didn't look good. We ran down a steep ramp and onto the beach. The morning was hot, the sand was soft, and the competition was fierce. I didn't think it was a race. However, I quickly realised that at a professional football club, when there were only 22 spots in the senior team and over 100 players vying for them, everything was a competition!

Running through soft sand on a hot day is bad enough. Running through soft sand on a hot day at a fierce pace when your fitness level is well below standard is another thing. We ran along the sand for what seemed to be an eternity, and then we came to another steep ramp. It was great to put my feet on solid ground despite the fact my legs felt like jelly. The relief was short-lived as we had to immediately run up this long and steep ramp. I had never experienced so much agony in my life to that point.

When we got to the top, I almost collapsed but thought to myself, I must keep going. Over the next few minutes, I recovered just enough to reach the next ramp, which took us back down to the beach to do it all over again. This stretch of sand was longer, softer, and more torturous than before. The good news was the beach was coming to an end with no ramp in sight. All I could see was a 100 metre (about 300 feet) vertical cliff. There was no way out. Surely that meant we would have to stop.

No such luck! We got to the bottom of this seemingly unassailable cliff and were instructed to climb it! I was shattered and on the verge of giving up. My legs were rubber, my lungs were on fire, and I could see no physical way to get to the top. In my mind, my thoughts were very much, *I can't do this.* Then, from behind, I heard: "Come on, Jobbas, you can do it". Some encouragement, finally! It was so welcoming. It planted the thought in my head that I could do this and spurred me on. I dug deeper into my resources to somehow claw my way to the top of the cliff.

I fell over at the top and then crawled on my hands and knees for a while until I somehow got back up onto my feet and stumbled down the road the final 1,000 metres and fell across the finish line. I honestly don't know if I would've made it to the top of the cliff or the end of the run without those few words of encouragement sowed into my mind and the following **thought and belief** I could do it.

After I got used to, and started enjoying, the pain of training, I began improving, and things started looking promising. Before I go further, I want to explore this idea of enjoying the pain and discomfort. I used to get asked all the time how I could possibly enjoy the pain and torture of the backbreaking and lung-busting training. You may be interested to know, my answer was this: "Simple, because I choose to love it". It is a deliberate thought process. Here was my thinking. My dream was to play senior professional football. To do that, I needed to be supremely fit and mentally strong. Therefore, every time I was pushed out of my comfort zone and into the torture zone, I knew I was getting fitter, stronger, and more mentally equipped. With every gut-busting session, I was getting closer to my dream. What's not to love about that? It's all in **how we think**!

As you stop and reflect on what I've just said, think about what you are currently doing or needing to do in your job, relationship, or life that's uncomfortable, painful and/or torturous. The key question is: if you do it, will it get you closer to the things you want in life? If so, stop negotiating it, stop avoiding it, stop making excuses, and start loving it. It's helping you achieve the dreams in your life. It's just a simple shift in thinking, and it will transform your life.

In my second year at St Kilda, I was seventeen years old. Because of my improvement, I gained selection to the senior reserve-grade team. Now I was playing with men. Big, strong, and fast men. Under normal circumstances, the reserve grade team would play before the senior team and on the same day. It was rarely televised because most people were only really interested in the senior team. However, on this occasion, my first senior-level reserve game would be televised live on a separate day.

The day came around, and the nerves were high. So too was the anticipation I could really make my mark and play a game that I would never forget. Ironically, it proved to be the case that this was a memorable game. I did make my mark, unfortunately, not for the reason I was hoping for. When the game started, it took me a while to find my feet. The game was faster than I was used to, the players were much bigger than I expected, and they most certainly hit harder than I was prepared for. Consequently, I spent most of the first quarter running around like a headless chicken, just trying to get myself into the game and avoid being run over. I eventually settled into the pace and started to get a couple of touches of the football.

By the end of the first quarter, I had survived, and I felt like I was coming to terms with the higher standard of football. I started the second quarter with more confidence and a strong feeling that something memorable would happen this quarter. It did, and it's a memory that haunts me every day and has done for around forty years (as I write this).

It was ten minutes into the quarter, and I was feeling comfortable and confident. I was on the centre wing, and the ball came out of defence and was kicked high in my direction. I thought: *Here's my chance. I'm going to take a spectacular mark and show everyone how good I really am.* The ball was high, and my eyes were firmly fixed on it. I was unaware I was surrounded by two opposing players, with another one steaming towards me. The ball came down, my hands wrapped around it and then everything went black!

The next thing I knew, I was on a stretcher, in the change rooms waiting for an ambulance to take me to the hospital, with a throbbing headache. I really had no idea what had just happened to me – all I knew was I had a very sore head. It wasn't until I watched the replay that I was horrified to see what happened to me. I'm glad I didn't see it coming and glad I didn't feel too much. I was unconscious in a heartbeat.

There is a video of this incident floating around on YouTube. So, if you feel the sadistic need to watch this replay and see a skinny and ill-equipped seventeen-year-old being crushed like an insect, you can do some searching through my channel. I hope you enjoy watching it as much as I *enjoyed* bringing it to you!

I spent the night in the hospital under close observation. I was discharged the next day with the strong recommendation of doctors and nurses to give up football. They warned me of the dangers. They condemned me for even participating in such a dangerous sport and then sent me on my way with an icy farewell.

I thought my only injury was a concussion, but as I got out of the hospital bed, I realised it was much more severe. As soon as I put the weight on my feet, my right knee buckled underneath me. What no one had realised, or been too concerned about at the time, was that when I was hit, I had seriously twisted my right knee as I fell to the ground. Now, not only was I nursing a seriously bashed head, but I also needed crutches to walk with. It would be fair to say I was not in great spirits, and I was now genuinely starting to question this whole football career dream.

Over the next few days, I had a decision to make. I had the condemning words of doctors and nurses ringing in my ears. I had the absolute concern of my mother and father to deal with, not to mention my own doubts and fears. It is a dangerous sport, and I was vulnerable because of my lack of physical prowess. So, what should I do? Do I gracefully bow out and justify it by saying I gave it a shot, but it just wasn't my *cup of tea*? It would have been an understandable decision. In that situation, most people would have agreed I was lucky I wasn't critically hurt and was doing the right thing. I must be honest and say I was very tempted.

My other choice was to get up and go again, which is clearly the decision I ultimately made. Sure, there's risk involved, but there's risk in everything. Despite the injury, I enjoyed the attention I got from everyone due to that incident. I still, to this day, enjoy showing people in seminars and talks the replay of such a memorable event and the powerful lesson of getting back up in 1982.

The final decision for me was an easy one. It came down to how badly I wanted to play professional football. I decided it was worth the pain, the fear, the occasional ambulance rides, and the disapproving opinions of other people. I got up and kept going and must tell you that I've been knocked down and got up many more times since. It's a **thought** and decision I will always be grateful I made and one which has shaped my life and achievements over the last forty years.

In the following year, a miracle occurred. I'm not sure it was really a miracle, or rather the thought I had and faith I held in my head that I would make it. It was the last game of the 1983 season, and I had been a good reserve-grade footballer all year. I was hoping that getting selected in the senior team would be realised during this particular year. However, I was okay even if it didn't because I knew, in my heart, it would happen.

It was the Saturday morning before the last game of the year, and I was getting ready for the early game in the second-grade team. The phone rang at about 8:00 am. *Who could that be?* I thought. I answered it and, whilst I recognised the voice, I was not prepared, so I couldn't connect the voice with the actual person.

It was the senior coach. He explained that several players could not play due to some injuries, so I was in the team! I tried to comprehend what just occurred, but I was shocked, amazed, excited, and ready. After a few minutes of stunned silence, I ran around the house screaming and woke everyone up. I won't go into all the details of that exciting day back in 1983. You can read more about it in my book *Kicking On*. What I will say is, at the time, I knew I had made it.

Well, it's an interesting principle in life that we don't always get what we want! However, I was prepared and excited that my senior professional career was now off and running. I was fit and ready for the first game of the next season and knew it was my time. I was wrong. I missed selection for the first and every game for the entire season, then the first half of the next season. In fact, it was twenty months from the first senior game in August 1983 until my next in April 1985.

So, you may be asking, what was it that kept me from having a tantrum, doubting myself and giving up at some point in those twenty months? I can tell you I came precariously close, many times. The thing that kept me going was a **thought** I kept repeating to myself every day, every training session, and after every missed selection. The thought was: *I will keep showing up.* In my mind, if I kept arriving, presenting, working, improving, and persisting, it would eventually pay off, or they would tell me I am not good enough. Either way, I would know for sure. I am so glad I hung in there and kept showing up because my career was officially launched after that second game in 1985.

I shudder to think what may have happened or where I would be today if I had succumbed to the strong desire to throw in the towel. I would never have had seven years of professional football. I honestly don't think I would be the person I am or enjoy the things I've achieved today. When people ask what the best time of my seven-year football career with St Kilda was, I always tell them it was those twenty months. Why? Because in that time, I got better, stronger, fitter, more resilient, mentally tougher, and more prepared for what professional football and life would, and will continue, to throw at me. I am a better person today because of those twenty months of frustration, discouragement, adversity, and growth. All because of the **thought**, *I will keep showing up.*

The final quick story I want to share in this chapter is a fast forward from the end of my professional football career, some fifteen years. Since the late 1980s, I worked hard in the fitness industry as a personal trainer and was at a crossroad in my life. I worked eighty hours a week, sacrificed many things and even lost many dollars in the process of trying to create success in my life. At the time, I was trying to remove myself from a tragically failing café business.

In 2002, I was sitting at my desk, head in my hands, wondering how I would survive and what I would do. I was in massive financial debt, worked crazy hours, had no life, and just wanted out! I had a vision in my heart to make a difference in the lives of others, and I had a dream to have multiple streams of income and not have to work as hard as I had been for so many years. About that time, and because of that vision, a **thought** dropped into my head. Where it came from, I don't know. Why I listened to it, again, I don't know. But boy, I'm glad it came and that I took notice of it!

The thought was illogical, irrational, and poorly timed. The thought was perfect! The thought was, *I should write a book.* Looking back, I now know it was God who put that thought into my head, but at that moment, I had no idea where it came from. Even though it made no sense at the time, I am so glad I listened to it.

I genuinely want you to understand the power of the thoughts you choose to focus on. This thought of mine was crazy, yet it became a reality. This thought of mine had no basis in logic or reasoning, yet it was fulfilled. This thought of mine was not backed up with any qualifications, experience, or previous desire, but I did it anyway. This thought was strong enough and clear enough for me to overcome all the time constraints, knowledge limitations and other forces working against me to get the job done. Most of all, this thought changed the whole direction of my life and started me on the path to a purposeful and abundant existence.

The result of that one crazy, illogical, yet powerful thought was I ended up writing a best-selling book. Within two years of being published, I retired as a personal trainer and became a full-time author. The things that have happened in my life since then have been incredible. If you don't already know, I have written eight books and created on-line programs and businesses. I have given presentations at corporate functions, schools, and public events. I mentor authors and have been on radio shows. The travel I have done, and even the people I have been blessed to meet, have come either directly or indirectly from that one seemingly irrational thought.

Can you see how important it is to choose to focus on the right thoughts? I'm talking about thoughts like: *I can; I'm good enough; I will find a way; I trust God; I have faith; I will improve; I will keep going; I am worthwhile; I am unique and special; I am here for a purpose; I fulfil my purpose; I love people; I am making a difference in the lives of others; I am changing my circumstances; I have control over my destiny; I take full responsibility; I am a winner.* There are many more positive and empowering thoughts.

It's a choice as to whether we select these thoughts. But be aware, it's almost easier and tragically more normal, to think the opposite thoughts like: *I can't; I'm not good enough; I will never find a way; I'm stuck and stupid; I will give up; I am not worthwhile; I am average and nothing special; I am a waste of space; I will never fulfil my purpose; I sceptical of people; I am making no difference in the lives of others; I can never change my circumstances; I have no control over my destiny; It's not my fault or responsibility; I am a loser.* There are many more negative and disempowering thoughts. Be aware, these thoughts will debilitate and devastate your life.

The wrong thoughts will move you to give up on something that could be the most amazing thing you will ever do. If you think you're not good enough, and stop trying, you will never know what could have been. The wrong thoughts around your health will take you down a dangerous eating and exercise path that will lead you to sickness, disease and, dare I say it, death. The wrong thinking will cause conflict, financial stress, frustration, and regret.

The great news is that it can all be changed in a heartbeat. As soon as you change your focus from disempowering to empowering, the whole domino effect will change direction. Before long, you will be on a path that will lead in a very different direction. One that will give you everything you want in life. So, take control of your thinking today.

Moving towards 'TEARS of Joy'

> Philippians 4:8 – *Finally, brothers and sisters, whatever is true, whatever is noble, whatever is right, whatever is pure, whatever is lovely, whatever is admirable – if anything is excellent or praiseworthy – think about such things.* (NIV)

I hope the message has been obvious enough in this chapter. I know I sometimes repeat myself, but there is no more important message for your life than this one. Please, take some time to look at the vision board you have created, and think about the faces of the people who give your life purpose. Imagine the life you want to live, visualise the things you want to achieve, and identify your thoughts. It is these current thoughts that will pretty much determine whether your vision becomes a reality or not. Please, be clear on that point.

Whatever you need to do to ensure your thoughts will start the 'TEARS of joy' process, please do it. The next chapter is devoted to ideas and strategies to help you start turning your thoughts into your greatest allies. With the right thinking and knowledge, anything is possible. I will talk in more detail about Oprah Winfrey later in the book, but right now, let me ask you a question. Do you think her astronomical impact, influence and success was the result of an affluent background? The fact was, she grew up in poverty and was raised by her grandmother whose greatest wish for her was to be treated kindly as a domestic worker in a wealthy home.

Oprah's incredible career, success and wealth are the result of the thoughts she started focusing on, and the life she started visualising, as a young girl. We can all do that. Are you ready to change the direction of your life? The right thoughts, beliefs, and perspectives, and trusting God, is the first step in helping you live the most amazing life available to you.

Key questions and action steps

1. What results are you getting in certain areas of your life?
2. What are the primary thoughts you focus on in each of these areas?
3. Can you identify why you are getting the results you are experiencing?
4. Think about the things you have strong and empowering thoughts about, and the things you have fearful and disempowering thoughts about. Why is that?
5. For the things you have disempowering thoughts and doubts about, can you come up with conclusive proof that you can't achieve them? This is something to think about with every fear or doubt you have.
6. Let's do a quick exercise that will help with what we will cover in the next chapter. Grab two sheets of paper. On one of them, I want you to list all the empowering thoughts you have about achieving your goals, dreams, and vision for your best life. On the other write down all the fears, doubts, and concerns you have about the process of achieving your goals, dreams, and best life. Which list is longer?
7. Just know that the longer list will win. Whatever predominating thoughts you hold in your mind will become a reality. So, if the longer list is the disempowering one, then get ready to change it. Okay?
8. Can I encourage you, whether a believer or not, to pray to God? Ask for the right thoughts about anything you are working on, aspiring to, or struggling with now? Then, when the answer comes, whether logical or not, act on it with faith that it will lead you where you want to be.

CHAPTER 7

Creating powerfully positive thoughts

"The Principle of the Path, says, it is direction, not intention which determines destination."

Let's get practical in this chapter. Suppose we understand the power of our thoughts, beliefs, and perspectives. They trigger a process that will move us either toward a 'TEARS of joy' type success, or a *tears of pain* type adversity. In that case, then focusing on the right thoughts is vital, right? This sounds simple, and it is, but it is certainly not easy. Why? Because many of our thoughts are not even conscious, they have been stored because of repetitive experiences, input, and thoughts. They now happily reside in our unconscious mind.

Before we get into the meat of this chapter, I want you to have a

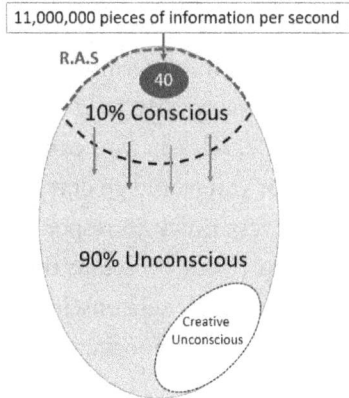

11,000,000 pieces of information per second

R.A.S

40

10% Conscious

90% Unconscious

Creative Unconscious

basic understanding of how your brain works. Keep in mind, I am an ex-footballer and have had my head beaten around a few times, so this is going to be a straightforward explanation. I hope you are okay with that. If you want a comprehensive and detailed understanding of how your brain works, this is not the book for you.

As you can see, my basic style diagram is shaped like a football. This helps me! In most human brains, only about ten per cent of the facts, information, beliefs, and memories are stored in the conscious mind. In fact, they are not really stored there. They are held there for long enough, and with enough repetition and reinforcement, until they are moved into your unconscious mind to be filed away, forever. In the unconscious mind, they clearly move out of your conscious thinking and into the part of the brain that stores ninety per cent of the facts, information, beliefs, and memories. Within the unconscious part of the brain resides the creative unconscious mind, and this is where most decisions are made. Isn't that interesting? Many decisions you make and actions you take are not even conscious to you. That makes sense, doesn't it? You may have asked yourself: *Why do I keep saying things like that? Why do I keep sabotaging myself? Why do I always procrastinate on things?* On the positive side, you also have wonderful unconscious habits, like brushing your teeth, eating breakfast, complimenting people, finding the good in all situations, and many other empowering rituals.

In simplified terms, your unconscious mind is like a room full of filing cabinets that hold all your experiences and memories for your whole life. Clearly, you cannot keep all information in your conscious mind, or you would go crazy. Inside this room is a very obedient servant who is very quick to respond to your signals, and digs up information to support your conscious thoughts. This servant feeds that information into the creative subconscious mind, and a decision is made. You control the decision by choosing the signals you send to this very loyal servant.

Let's look at one situation and two possible scenarios. John Snoogelhorjn is heavily overweight and, after many failed attempts, has decided to try again to restore his health and wellbeing. John's conscious thinking, and the thoughts he chooses to focus on, will determine what outcomes he gets from this next attempt at getting himself back to great health and wellbeing.

Scenario one. As soon as John sets a goal to regain his life, improve his energy, and lose excess body fat, he has what he believes are harmless thoughts like: *I don't know if I can do it;* or *I will probably give up like the times before.* The instant he has these conscious thoughts, a message is sent to the obedient servant in the unconscious mind. This servant goes to work to sort through the files and come up with all the evidence to support why John <u>cannot</u> achieve his goal, and why he will probably give up. It comes up with all the times in John's life that he has failed in his attempts and has given up on things. This information is sent to the creative unconscious mind, and a decision is automatically made. Without John even realising it, he has just sabotaged another attempt to restore his health and wellbeing.

Scenario two. This time, as soon as John sets the goal to regain his life, improve his energy, and lose excess body fat, he chooses quite different thoughts: *I know I can do this;* or *My past is not my future;* or *I am determined, focused, and can quickly regain my lean and fit body and optimal health and energy.* The instant he has these conscious thoughts, a message is sent to the loyal servant in the unconscious mind who goes to work to diligently sort through the files and come up with all the evidence to support why John <u>can</u> achieve his goal, and why he will be successful. It comes up with all the times in John's life that he has succeeded in his attempts and persisted on things. This information is sent to the creative unconscious mind, and a decision is automatically made. Without John even realising it, he has just set himself up for an exciting and successful life of health and vitality.

So, let's go back to the diagram of the brain. We live in an over-stimulated world. There are signals, words, voices, sounds, smells, tastes, textures, sights, and other bits of information coming at us from every angle. I mean, if you were to stop now and just take in every piece of information from the world around you, you would go crazy trying to process it all. In fact, from my understanding, around 11 million pieces of information bombard your brain through your eyes, ears, nose, mouth and touch every second. As I said, if you tried to process all of them, your brain would explode.

Luckily, you have a filter to sort through and direct only the relevant information into your conscious mind. This filter is called the RAS or Reticular Activating System. The RAS identifies the relevant and important information to you based on your values and the things you are giving attention to. You have undoubtedly heard the analogy of when you decide you want to buy a particular car. Suddenly, you see the exact car on the road everywhere, and out of nowhere, there seems to be more of those cars on the road. Are there? No, it is simply that your RAS is bringing them to your conscious attention.

Of the 11 million pieces of information per second, your RAS filters and directs only around forty of the most relevant pieces per second into your conscious mind. This is much more manageable than 11 million. The information goes into your conscious mind to be analysed and interpreted based on your orientation towards life, the meanings you apply, and whether you are happy, sad, positive, negative, resentful, grateful, victim-minded, or solution-oriented. You see, everything that happens, and every piece of information that goes into the conscious mind, can be determined as good or bad.

Here are some examples. Imagine you are stuck in a traffic jam. In that case, you will either get angry and frustrated because you will be late, or grateful and excited you get more time to listen to the positive audio playing. If someone says something unkind to you, you can react by being insulted, angry, lashing out, or respond with empathy as they are obviously going through a tough time. If your weight increases, you will be upset, discouraged, give up, or be intrigued and even more determined to get your weight to the desired point.

I am assuming a happy and successful life is what we all aspire to. In that case, we need to take a positive, solution-oriented and possibility approach to each piece of information our RAS allows to enter our conscious mind. This can only happen if we control the thoughts, beliefs and attitudes that move from the limited space in the conscious mind to the larger storage facility in the unconscious mind. The more positive thoughts, beliefs, and attitudes stored in the unconscious filing system, the more resources the servant will retrieve and direct to the creative subconscious mind. Therefore, the more positive, powerful, and transformational decisions we will make and actions we will take. I hope all that makes sense. That is about as clinical, scientific, and detailed as I can get. Now, my head is about to explode!

The most important thing you can learn, and what I talk about most in this chapter, is how to develop more positive thoughts, beliefs, and attitudes in our conscious mind. When you understand that and act, you move them into the place where they will have the most wonderful impact on your unconscious storage facility and your life. Get ready for the most life-changing chapter you have ever read. That is, if you act on the information.

Make no mistake about it. If you apply it with faith and consistently, the information I am about to share will change your life, as it has mine. For a while, and until it becomes habitual, it will take time and focus. It will not always be fun or comfortable. A little bit of work for a long and happy life of wellness and wonder. Are you up for it? If you said yes, let's do this.

Just know your unconscious mind is already full of information, knowledge, facts, and beliefs you have accumulated over your whole life.

Depending on the source and orientation of that information, you are currently living your life and operating based on the mental programs established in your unconscious mind over many years. Remember the fourteen-year-old boy I discussed in Chapter 2 who declared to 200 of his fellow students that he was dumb. He is not dumb, and was not born with that belief. I know nothing about his life story. I do know the idea was planted in his head and reinforced many times in his life, to that point. Maybe it was his parents, his siblings, and even perhaps well-meaning teachers. Who knows? It doesn't matter. What matters is it led to a firmly entrenched belief he is dumb, which has and will play out repeatedly in his life if he doesn't do something to change it.

My point is this. Years of reinforcement have led you to believe many things. Some things are useful and will help you live an amazing life, but some things will stop you and potentially lead you down a very unsavoury path. To change disempowering and limiting beliefs, you need to apply the same process and routine that got them there first, and replace them with positive, powerful, and uplifting beliefs. My point, again, is it will take time, persistence, patience, and consistency.

Let's look at five ways you can start to move positive and powerful beliefs and thoughts from your conscious into your unconscious mind. They are repetition, desire, faith, present thinking, and what you really want.

Repetition

Everything you currently believe is the result of repetition. If you were told, for the first time, as a child, you were dumb, you would probably not believe it. In fact, if you were told, for the first time, as a child, you were the smartest person alive, you would probably not believe that either. However, if the message was repeated to you every day, from a range of sources, then over time, it would become part of your internal and unconscious belief system. Interestingly, we will believe things that have no basis in reality or truth if we are exposed to them for long enough with constant repetition. To believe you are dumb, not talented enough, or unable to achieve certain things is a big fat lie! It has just been reinforced to you so many times you now believe it. It can be changed.

You may not know about the power and impact of the simple things you are exposed to each day. Things like the people you hang around, television, radio, music and reading material. They all significantly influence your belief system. People who watch television shows based on violence, fear, bad news, and crime are, over time, and with repetition, becoming conditioned to that way of thinking and believing. In fact, if you think about your favourite television show as a child, I bet you can sing the theme song, and you know the words, off by heart. Am I right?

I was listening to an inspirational speaker a few years ago who was talking about this very subject. Without any warning, he asked the audience to sing with him the theme song for *Gilligan's Island*. Keep in mind this talk was a while ago when the main generation in the audience had grown up with *Gilligan's Island*. You know the television shows you grew up with and watched each day. I bet you also could sing along with the words of the theme songs. So, this guy starts singing the *Gilligan's Island* theme song, and the whole audience, including me, sang with him. We could all sing it, from memory, word for word.

His point, as is mine, is this. At what moment did anyone deliberately decide they were going to learn those words? Never, right? So, how does everyone know them? Simply because of repetition. His next point was very powerful. He said: "*If something is going to be in there. If something is going to be sent to the unconscious mind. If Gilligan's Island, The Brady Bunch, The Love Boat, Friends, Big Bang Theory, or whatever theme song you have in your memory is going to be there, then why not deliberately put in something that is going to change your life for the better forever?*"

Right now, like me, you have some negative and limiting beliefs controlling your life, and they came about over time and with repetition. That being the case, what if you could start to overpower those beliefs with new positive and empowering ones, and transform your life? The first activity I want to share relates to something I did to help myself overcome my many limiting beliefs about becoming a successful author. I use it regularly whenever I feel fear, insecurity, and doubt creep in.

1. When I thought about holding my own published book in my hands, I was incredibly excited but still felt anxiety, doubt, and fear.
2. On a sheet of paper, I wrote a list of the causes of that anxiety, doubt, and fear. In other words, I wrote down the challenges and obstacles I felt were going to be a barrier to writing my book. Things including: *I have no time;* and *I am not a writer.*
3. I looked at each one of those limiting beliefs and asked myself: *Is that what I want?*
4. On <u>another sheet of paper</u>, I clearly wrote **what I wanted** for each one. Using the two examples above, I wrote: *I easily prioritise the time I need to write my book because it is important to me,* and *I am a successful writer who inspires and engages people all around the world.*
5. As I went through my entire list of negatives, I created a list of powerful, positive, and present-tense affirming statements.
6. Now, the fun bit. I took that first sheet of paper, the one with all the negative, yucky limiting beliefs on it, and tore it into little pieces. As I destroyed it, I said: *Goodbye, you will never hold me back again. You are gone from my life forever.* Then I threw it away. As it went into the garbage can, I immediately felt lighter. The heaviness of those negative beliefs was gone.

7. I then committed to reading these new positive affirmations to myself. I looked in the mirror <u>every day</u>, even when I didn't feel like it and didn't believe it. This was and is the key to my success as an author and other areas of my life.

My experience has reinforced that repetition absolutely works, although some things I have chosen to do may sound a little extreme. To have what I wanted, and live the life I dreamt of, I needed to significantly increase the repetition of positive input and reduce the repetition of negative input. I stopped watching the news and current affairs programs on the television. I stopped listening to the radio. I stopped reading the newspaper, books, and other material that were not lifting and inspiring me. Why stop? Because it was the repetition of bad news, gossip, and negativity in the world that was filtering into my brain and feeding my unconscious mind.

Therefore, I decided to feed it with great stuff that would filter through and uplift, encourage, empower, and inspire me. I started doing something I wish I had done years before. I started reading. I committed to at least fifteen minutes every day to reading books that would empower and educate me. I started listening to positive audios and podcasts when I was driving in my car. I only watched television that would uplift me and make me feel good. I started to regularly attend educational, informative, and inspirational seminars and events. I started speaking to my mentor every morning, Monday to Friday. Doing this made such a difference.

Over the last few years, and as I have already mentioned, my powerful and positive repetition started to include my faith-based activities. I now pray to God every morning for thanks, for forgiveness, and for what I want in my life. I began listening to worship songs every morning as I took my dog, Joia, for her walk. I started reading a chapter of the Bible every day. Let me tell you, the Bible is the oldest and best personal development book. I started attending church once, sometimes twice a week, and associating with other wonderful people. This addition to my life has been the rocket fuel that has propelled me over the last few years.

The result of all this powerful and positive repetition facilitated a positive change in my life very quickly. Many people cannot understand why, but when you think about it, it is obvious. I read fifteen minutes per day, which is over 91 hours per year, and leads me to read about one book a month or an additional twelve books per year. I average one to two, sometimes three positive audio inputs per day. This is at least one hour per day, and equates to a minimum of 365 hours per year or an extra fifteen days of positive input. This does not include the events I attend or the positive shows I watch, which would equate, on average, to another hour per day or fifteen full days per year.

In addition, I speak to my mentor for ten minutes each morning, which equates to more than 43 hours per year. I invest over four hours per week into my spiritual regime, equating to over 225 hours, or nine days per year. The total of this wonderful repetition and reinforcement comes close to 1,000 hours, or 41 days per year of empowering input. Can you see how repetition, when focused on the right things, can dramatically change your life? I started dealing with situations better, saying things that often surprised me (and still do) and achieving more than I ever had. This happened through the deliberate repetition of positive thoughts, words, ideas, beliefs, and faith, I fed into my conscious mind, which then moved into my unconscious mind.

Desire

Let's face it, and as you now know, nothing moves without desire. Without an emotional charge or compelling desire, a thought will evaporate like a drop of water on a hot stovetop. Suppose you have forced yourself to do positive affirmations without really feeling the words you are saying, or imagining the exciting reality of what you are talking about. In that case, they will go in and straight back out again. To be effective and transformational, this is not a mechanical process. This is where we, as humans, have the most amazing advantage over all other creatures. We are emotional beings. Of course, sometimes we allow those emotions to work against us. However, when we can harness them, they will turn a mere sentence into a powerful and unstoppable commitment to achieve what many believe is unachievable. This is emotional desire.

Petrea King is a best-selling author, speaker, and founder of the *Quest for Life Foundation*. A cancer survivor herself, Petrea and the team at *Quest for Life* help many people going through all forms of trauma, and have been doing so for many decades. I had the incredible privilege of speaking to her on my podcast in 2021. She was diagnosed with a very aggressive form of acute myeloid leukaemia in 1983, and given only three months to live. Now 38 years on from that diagnosis, she is passionate, purposeful, and still going strong.

In the podcast called *Weep the tears*, I asked her how she was able to overcome such a devasting diagnosis and still be thriving almost forty years later. Her answer surprised and delighted me. She said: "I wept, and I sobbed for weeks, and I released all of the pent-up emotion inside of me". Once she had released the fear, anger, and bitterness that was ruling her life, she focused on the life that was meaningful for her. She had a powerful desire to make a difference in the life of others, and she has been joyfully living that life ever since.

In my teens, and without even realising it, my thoughts, visualisation, and goal to be a professional footballer were packaged up in a burning desire with a strong emotional pull. For me, the achievement came not just because of the words I affirmed or the pictures I imagined but, importantly, the feelings that went with them. When I said to myself, *I am a successful footballer in front of thousands of screaming fans,* I could feel the emotions really happening. I could feel the excitement of running onto the ground through the banner to the roar of the crowd. I could feel the adrenaline pumping through my body as I grabbed the ball and did something wonderful, causing the crowd to rise to their feet. I could feel the pride and satisfaction of my accomplishments with every thought and mental image. It was an emotionally charged desire that moved me to achieve my goal, not just the repetition of words, thoughts, and pictures.

One of my current goals is to live in Europe and/or the USA. I have a vision board, and I affirm it every day, but that is not why it will happen. It will happen because I am not just mechanically going through the motions. It will happen because every time I look at pictures or do my affirmations, I am reminiscing on my visit to the USA in 2019 and Italy in 2018. I am re-living the emotion of being there. I can see the sights, feel the warm breeze on my face and smell the typically American and Italian smells. I can feel the warm breeze on my face as I walk on Venice Beach, or through the Cinque Terre. I am excited about the lives I will impact and the global influence I will have. I feel the love, the pride, and the excitement of what I have created for myself. This emotional desire moves me to get the job done, and it is the same emotion that will drive you to success when added to your repetition.

There are some things you can do to unleash desire. Here are some ideas to increase the power of repetition, allow powerful positive thoughts to slide into your unconscious mind, and power up your life:

1. Create your vision board and describe an ideal day. Add pictures that move you and those that really connect you emotionally to the day and life you want to live. Get clear on your purpose and what is most important to you, and make sure what you do every day is moving you towards it and helping you enjoy it more.

2. Be clear on the faces in your life who give your vision and journey meaning. When you think of those faces, do they evoke a strong emotional response?

3. Each day look at your vision and description, close your eyes and imagine it happening. Really allow yourself to sink into the moment and experience those wonderful feelings of pride, excitement, joy, and fulfilment. These feelings will help create the desire to move these thoughts and visions to play a more positive active role in your life.

4. Add an emotional component to the affirmations you created for yourself. Let us look at the affirmation example: *I easily prioritise the time I need to write my book because it is important to me.* Let's beef it up a little with something to trigger a strong emotional response: *I easily prioritise the time I need to write my book because I feel the need to impact the world and create financial freedom.* Suppose you are trying to get health back, and you have children. In that case, you may affirm something like – *It feels incredible to be lean and healthy. I am excited to set a positive example for my children to live a healthy and happy life.* If you are a parent and something like that does not move you emotionally, I am not sure what will!

5. The words you use daily will help you feel and establish these positive emotions. Use words that are big, powerful, and positive. When someone asks you how you are, say: *I am fantastic and getting better.* When someone asks you what you do, say: *I am so grateful and excited to be able to...* When you are describing things, use words like *awesome, brilliant, incredible, and amazing.* These words immediately help you feel more positive and empowered.

I recently spoke to a group of young divers striving for a high level of achievement in the sport. They ranged from eight to fifteen years old, and we were talking about mindset and goal achievement and working through the 'TEARS of joy' model. After we had worked backwards from **Success** to **Thoughts**, I asked if there were any questions. One of the older girls put her hand up and asked me how she could be more motivated to do the training and push herself to reach the next level. It was an interesting question, and it reinforced to me the power of this emotional connection to influence the thought and really make it zing.

She was suffering from one or both of two barriers. The first barrier was the diving dream was not hers. Maybe it was coming from her parents who wanted to see her be successful, however, not something she had a passionate desire about. The other possible barrier is she had not yet connected the work to the achievement and then to the bigger picture. I suspect that was the problem. It is so easy to get caught up in the discomfort of the process we lose sight of the life we are striving for. In both scenarios, she had lost her emotional connection to the thoughts and affirmations she was saying. They had no power or strength because they were not backed by a powerful and compelling emotional pull.

Faith

There are some wonderful definitions, descriptions, and perceptions of the word faith, and I will just share two of them with you. As a newly born-again Christian, I love the passage from the Bible in Hebrews 11:1, which states: *'Faith is the substance of things hoped for, the evidence of things not yet seen'*. The other I want to share is from the author, Philip Yancey, who says: *'faith means trusting in advance what will only make sense in reverse'*.

Let's just spend a little bit of time on both definitions. They may not make a lot of sense on the surface, but they are incredibly profound and powerful when you dig in and really understand them. In fact, they are life-changing. There are two pieces to the passage from Hebrews I initially did not understand at all. *'Faith is the substance of things hoped for.'* What does that mean? Now I feel I have a better handle on this scripture. I understand what it is saying and, wow, it is a game-changer if you believe it and act. Effectively, it is saying that hope without faith has no substance. Hope is a wonderful thing to have, as it keeps people enduring and surviving in times of adversity. However, it is not a strategy for success unless you add in faith. Faith brings hope to life. Faith converts hope from a wish to a possibility, probability or even certainty, depending on your level of faith. Faith gives hope the substance to create reality.

The second part of the verse says *'the evidence of things not yet seen'*. Again, if you understand the significance of this statement and believe it is true, it will change your life. Remember, hope is wanting something you do not know if you will ever have. You might say things like: *I hope it rains today; I hope I get the job; I hope I get better;* and *I hope to become an author.* When you add the faith component, it provides <u>evidence</u> it will happen, even if you have no idea how. Faith is a force that sits outside logical thinking, and firmly in possibility, even miracle, thinking.

It was faith that allowed David to slay Goliath when all logic said it was not possible. Faith allowed Jesus to raise Lazarus four days after he died and was rotting in a cave. My faith was the main resource I applied to become an author and do the things I am doing today. Faith is the substance that gives hope power, and it provides the evidence to believe in the things you cannot yet see. A common saying is that *'seeing is believing'*, but faith works on the premise that *'believing is seeing'*.

The other quote, by Phillip Yancey, says: *'faith means trusting in advance what will only make sense in reverse'*. Trust is a big word and concept. Many people do not trust easily without evidence and reinforcement over time. So how does it make sense to trust something that has not happened and is not logical? For many people it sounds totally absurd to start in the process of achieving something without any idea of whether you can do it, or how to go about it. The reality is, though, I am sure you have experienced it at least once in your life. Think back to when you passed the test, published the book, got the job, made the team, got the girl or boy, or whatever it may be. When you look back on the unlikely journey, did it make sense? Even though you may have had no idea of how you were going to do it, the path unfolded for you, right? That is totally true for many of the things I have achieved in my life. The secret was, and is, faith.

As a Christian, I am taught, and I believe, if I accept that Jesus' life was given and His blood spilt to forgive me of my sins, I am divinely led and have the power of God to guide me to success and make a difference in this world. I can tell you it gives me incredible peace of mind. It absolutely helps me create impenetrable unconscious belief in my ability to create 'TEARS of joy'. As I affirm what I want, I do it knowing God is with me and will never lead me astray.

Now, I am not trying to preach to you, or convince you to do what I have done, unless you are open to it. I do, however, want to encourage you to find an unbreakable faith in something. Whether your faith is in Jesus, Allah, Buddha, the Universe, followers of The Force, intuition, or any other faith, I believe faith will help you achieve your dreams in life. If it can do that, why not investigate it?

How does faith work? It removes stress, anxiety, and fear. It helps us know and believe what we want is a done deal, and whatever we firmly decide and take consistent action on will happen, no doubts. If you are a sceptic, as I was, the best analogy I can use to explain this is with sport. As you know, I am a former professional footballer and, for many years of my life, football was everything. Even after I left the St Kilda Football Club, I still watched and followed the team closely.

There were times when I could not watch a live match, so I would record the game to watch later in the day. I didn't look at the scores because I simply did not want to know. I wanted to watch and imagine it was happening live. Trying to avoid finding out the scores was difficult because it was on the news, in the newspapers, and on the grapevine. On one occasion, I made the mistake of answering the call from a friend, a diehard St Kilda supporter, just before I went home to watch the replay. He could not help himself as he said: "That game was amazing. I still can't believe we actually won it!" Before I could stop him, it was out, and I knew the result.

I was disappointed to know, but excited we had won, so I went home to watch the game anyway. Generally, before a game, I have a lot of nervous energy, but before this game, I was calm. I settled in, got some refreshments, turned on the television and hit play to start watching the game. The game started, and my team was terrible in the first quarter. They had made mistake after mistake and had many goals kicked against them. Was I upset? Was I angry? Was I tense? Nope, I was very calm. Why? Because I knew the result. In the second quarter, my team was even worse. We got further and further behind and, by half-time, it seemed almost out of reach. Was I yelling at the television with high stress levels and frustration? Not at all, because I was certain of the result.

The game continued. My team fought back in the second half and somehow got over the line to win the game. Was it tense, stressful and heart-pumping? No, it was not. It was a relaxing and enjoyable afternoon of football because we won the game. I could simply relax with certainty because I knew the result. This is what faith is and feels like. As Philip Yancey says: *'faith means trusting in advance what will only make sense in reverse'*.

Faith gives power to your thoughts. Faith fuels your belief. Faith creates certainty and peace of mind. Faith will absolutely help you build and positively reprogram your unconscious mind. So, here are a couple of ideas to help you utilise this powerful concept.

1. The first step is to investigate, identify with, and submit to a faith that resonates with you. For much of my life I was, and still am, a true believer that the Universe delivers everything we give our focus, attention, and efforts to. I had faith in that. I now have a strong faith my success and destiny are guided by God. It may be something different for you, and it does not matter as long as you can find a source you can have faith in. I want to encourage you to spend some time reflecting, researching, and deciding to go down this path.

2. Can you achieve success in life without having a strong faith in something? Maybe, I'm not sure, but my attitude was if having faith will make it easier and more fulfilling, why not give it a go and just have faith. I know it sounds naïve, but it is working for me. So, once you have decided on what your faith will be, submit to it fully, or you are wasting your time.

3. Every time you have a thought, make an affirmation, read a book, listen to positive audio, or get advice from a mentor or a positive influence in your life, have faith. Trust that the words and beliefs will be moving into your unconscious mind and become a part of who you are and what you will do in life.

4. Practice this faith daily.

Present thinking

This is a simple one – not easy, but simple – and requires mindfulness and awareness of your current thoughts. As you know, your brain is on the go twenty-four-seven. You are talking to yourself every second of your waking hours, and even while you are sleeping. If you pay no attention to your thoughts, they will just move like a leaf in a stream and go with the flow. If you are anything like I was before I started to take my thoughts captive, I would just allow them to spiral.

Let's say something happened – like I received a rejection note from a publisher. Without deliberate attention, my thinking would start harmlessly enough but would go something like this:

> *Oh, that is a shame. I was hoping a publisher would be interested.*
>
> *I wonder why they rejected it. I thought it was good. Maybe it is not good enough.*
>
> *Am I wasting my time? Maybe I should try something else.*
>
> *I am kidding myself. How could I possibly think a footballer could be an author?*
>
> *I am such an idiot for thinking I could ever get published.*
>
> *I will give up and move on. At least I gave it a go.*
>
> *I am just not good enough.*

Have you ever let your thinking go down a path like that? Well, just know every one of those thoughts is re-affirming and cementing the belief that I am not good enough. So, guess what is being moved into my unconscious mind? You get the picture, right? Remember, you are in total control of the thoughts you hold on to, and you get to choose how you respond to any and everything that happens. If you can believe things happen for you, and not to you, you will find this process much easier. If I paid attention and genuinely believed everything does happen for me, let's see how this internal chatter could and should have gone and what it does for me now?

Oh, that is a shame. I was hoping a publisher would be interested.

That is okay. That publisher was probably not the right one for me anyway.

I will see what I can learn from the rejection and use it to refine and improve my next submission.

I know this process may take a while, and I am willing to keep going until I find the perfect publisher for me.

I am excited because my book is great, and it will be published.

I will keep going. The next publisher I submit to will be the right one.

I am making a massive difference in this world.

Can you see the difference? All it takes is conscious awareness and deliberate choice. Imagine if you can be just as certain in your belief that something great will come from every situation and circumstance. In that case, you will find taking control of your present thoughts an easy and powerful thing to do.

What you really want

This is such a simple thing, yet one that is so rarely considered by many people. You would imagine it easy to think about and focus on what you really want. If so, why do we experience fear, anxiety, doubt, anger, and confusion? If we focus on what we want, why are we still living well short of what is possible? These are interesting questions to ponder and, I can tell you, in most cases it is because we far too often think about what we do not want rather than what we do want.

In the past, I was quite an anxious person. I would wake up every morning with an uneasy, even stressed, feeling in my gut. I would not be excited about my day at all, and I just wanted to hit the snooze button and go back to sleep. Why? Simple, I was thinking about what I did not want. Probably the worst time for me was a year or two after I finished my teaching degree. I did not even realise I would be a teacher until the third year of the degree. Yes, it is true; my eyes and brain were football-shaped at that time of my life. I did not want to teach. It was not my passion. I hated trying to convince teenagers to learn algebra and trigonometry, and it caused me anxiety.

Every day my alarm went off, I would think about what I did not want:

> *I do not want to get up.*
> *I do not want to teach those little brats.*
> *I do not want to have to discipline them.*
> *I do not want to have to go to more boring meetings.*
> *I just do not want to be doing this.*

Can you imagine the type of mindset I was creating and the attitude I was developing with this type of thinking? I lasted four years in teaching. For much of those four years, I was in this debilitating thinking spiral. Ironically or not, it was also in this period I was sacked from the St Kilda Football Club. Wow, even as I am writing this, I am coming to an epiphany that maybe these events were linked. Maybe my teaching experience and focus on what I did not want affected my attitude and unconscious mind, translating into the approach I took to into my football career. Can you see how powerful what we focus on is and how it will impact our whole life?

After my sacking from the football club I went into a period of victim-thinking, and a very unhealthy blame mentality. I blamed the club, the coaches, the other players, the supporters, my lack of physical prowess. I even blamed my teaching job, which I was not enjoying. Looking back, I was so misguided and clueless. I was blaming the things I had previously negotiated and overcome to make it to the top level. I just needed a reason and justification for why I was sacked because I was not ready to take responsibility for my own thoughts, emotions, and actions.

After a period of self-pity, tantrums, victim-thinking, and misery, I decided it was no way to live my life, and it was time to change. I asked myself: *what do I want?* I really did want to teach and inspire people to be better. In my mind, the difference from my teaching job was I desired to work with people who wanted to be taught and were inspired by me. At that time of my life, teaching teenagers was not it. Ironically, thirty years later, I speak to teenagers in schools and am loving it. This may be because I am not a *teacher*. I can go in, connect with teenagers, have a positive impact, and leave when I want.

At that time, I obviously decided the teaching profession was not for me. I wanted to work in a gym because I loved sport and fitness. It was not long before I resigned from my teaching job and started working full-time in a gym. It was the beginning of an amazing journey that led to fifteen years of passionate application to personal training and the incredible things I am doing now and loving.

The decision to focus on what I wanted to do changed my life for the better almost immediately. When my thinking was directed at what I wanted, my outlook on life was more optimistic. My actions and attitudes changed and, not surprisingly, I started getting quite different results. The first full-time job I had in the gym lasted four to six months which led me to another full-time gym position for the following two years. This job opened my eyes to the idea of personal training. This led me to meet a man who enabled me to get started on my fifteen-year personal training journey. This was the catalyst for me writing my first book, and the rest, as they say, is history. All because I simply started focusing on what I wanted instead of what I did not want.

Moving towards 'TEARS of Joy'

> Proverbs 4:20-27 – *My son, pay attention to what I say; turn your ear to my words. Do not let them out of your sight, keep them within your heart; for they are life to those who find them and health to one's whole body. Above all else, guard your heart, for everything you do flows from it. Keep your mouth free of perversity; keep corrupt talk far from your lips. Let your eyes look straight ahead; fix your gaze directly before you. Give careful thought to the paths for your feet and be steadfast in all your ways. Do not turn to the right or the left; keep your foot from evil.* (NIV)

The critical part of achieving the success you want, and 'TEARS of joy', is the thoughts and thinking that you choose to focus on and hold on to. It starts the dominos falling and determines the direction in which they tumble. A wonderful quote by a pastor, speaker, and author, Andy Stanley, out of his book *The Principle of the Path* says: '*it is direction, not intention which determines destination*'. In other words, what you want and the results you long for are irrelevant if you do not choose the thoughts and take the actions that will lead you there. The actions you take are determined by your emotional state, which is based on the thoughts you choose to focus on. Do you get it? This part of the 'TEARS of joy' concept is critical because it determines the direction.

I have outlined many strategies in this chapter to help you focus on the right thoughts, and move them from your conscious to your unconscious mind. Start slowly. Pick the strategy that most resonates with you, and get to work. Will it be easy? Not always. Will there be times you feel like it is not working? Absolutely. Will you get pulled back towards your natural way of thinking? You can bank on it. Will it change your life for the better forever? It absolutely will if you stick to it.

Key questions and action steps

1. Do you have any awareness of the thoughts affecting your life, good or bad, which have moved into the unconscious part of your brain?
2. Spend some time and make a list of all the thoughts you regularly have that negatively impact your life in some way.
3. Which ones are having the greatest impact?
4. Are you ready to ensure your thoughts move you in the direction you want to go?
5. Choose at least one of the strategies I have discussed in this chapter and start the process of moving different thoughts into your unconscious mind.

CHAPTER 8

Nothing moves
without emotion

*"I love being emotional. In fact, I'm
emotional about being emotional!"*

To say that our willingness to manage our emotional state will have
the greatest impact on our lives is the understatement of the century.
Every decision we make, and every action we take, is based on an emotion or a feeling. In the classic Australian movie, *The Castle*, the clueless
solicitor Dennis Denuto says it this way: "It's the vibe of the thing". We
may back decisions up with our own justified version of logic but, the
reality is for the most part, the choice leading to any action is based on
a feeling. By the way, this is a feeling we created because of thoughts we
chose to keep in our mind and focus on. Make no mistake, our emotions
will either move us up to the most amazing joy and abundance possible
or down to destruction and pain you can't even imagine.

Have you ever done something you knew was the wrong thing to do,
then justified it with as many logical reasons you could come up with
to make it sound plausible to others? We have all done that. As much as

we may try to deny it, we need to realise and admit that emotion was the trigger for the decision. Rarely is it logic or reason. I mean, when you really can't afford to spend the money, what would be the reason for purchasing something you really don't need, like the largest and most hi-tech flat-screen TV you can buy? It is 100 per cent for the feeling associated with ownership, and sitting on your comfy couch watching your favourite movie or sporting event on a TV most people don't have. You may justify it by saying you needed to fill the blank space on a wall, but we all know that logic can't explain the purchase.

Have you ever said something to someone in the heat of an emotional moment you later regretted? Surely, we all have. However, before the regret and the realisation that it was the wrong thing to say kicked in, you logically justified to yourself why you said it. It was because they deserved it, or they needed to learn the lesson, or it wasn't your fault because they made you angry. Isn't that classic? *It wasn't my fault, they made me angry!* It's time we all grew up and took responsibility for our own emotional state, our own words, and our actions. People don't make us angry. We choose anger based on the thoughts we focus on from the situation. Are you getting my drift here?

This may be difficult to read because it places responsibility for all your thoughts, emotions, and actions firmly on your shoulders and mine. No longer can you say *it's not my fault I lashed out. John made me angry.* Stop blaming John. You chose to focus on the thought that led to anger. From here on you can't say: *I am so upset my weight hasn't gone down, I had to eat the chocolate bar.* You can blame the scales, the gym, your personal trainer, or the chocolate bar as much as you like. However, you chose to romance the thought that led to feeling upset, and <u>you</u> put the chocolate bar in your own mouth.

Two weeks after playing in a grand final with St Kilda, when I read about my sacking in the newspaper, my thoughts led to the emotions that caused me to do things I still regret. The fact I found out I was sacked by reading it in the newspaper was wrong. There is no excuse for the lack of courtesy and professionalism of the football club. However, the reason for my sacking fell squarely on my shoulders and my actions leading to that moment. It was my fault that my immature and underdeveloped emotional intelligence took me down the victim-thinking-blame-everyone-but-me path. My erroneous thinking led to strong emotions causing me to do and say things I have and will always regret. It destroyed my chance to further my professional sporting career.

That's enough of the negative impact of emotional stuff, agree? Let's explore the positive and powerful effects of emotions caused by focusing on the right thoughts.

The reality is that nothing moves without emotion. The word originated many centuries ago from the Latin word *emovere*, meaning to move out, remove and/or agitate. This came from the assimilated form of *ex*, meaning out, and *movere*, meaning to move. I like the word agitate. It's where I am right now, and hence why I'm writing this book. In my mind, emotion means *agitate into motion*. As I looked in the thesaurus for other words, like agitate, *excite* was one of them. So, we could also describe emotion as *excite into motion*.

I have already talked about Deborah Stathis who created an incredible transformation in her life. After a horrendous car accident, she defied every medical odd against her to create a new and improved version of herself. Looking at her today, you would never know she has an acquired brain injury, or that she broke her nose, lower jaw, upper jaw, cheekbones, forehead, and skull base (which the brain sits on).

So, the question on many people's lips is: how did she do it? I will answer that in six simple words. She harnessed the power of emotion! What do I mean? In her book *Beyond Trauma*, and in her podcast conversations with me, she described the situation in the rehabilitation centre when she chose to look at her damaged and disfigured face in the mirror. At that moment, she turned to the mirror, eyes down to the floor, and slowly lifted her head to examine the face that was, at that time, her reality. She looked, she felt intense emotion, and she sobbed.

As you can imagine, initially, the emotion was extreme sadness for finding herself in this situation. Soon afterwards, the emotion turned to fear that the disfigured and brain-damaged person she was looking at in the mirror could be who she would be for the rest of her life. After stopping and reflecting, she asked herself this very powerful question: *You are here now, what are you going to do?* This question sparked a vision of what she wanted: overcoming this trauma and living a normal life. This focus on what she wanted triggered what she describes as a *relentless determination and pursuit* to live a successful and abundant life. She then harnessed the power of this strong desire to beat every medical forecast, and then, from that moment, she did whatever she needed to do. Whilst it was a tough journey at times, she never relented. This, my friend, is the power of emotion.

As I look back, I have been excited and agitated into motion throughout my life by thoughts I have held onto and focused on. The absolute excitement got me from the thought of being a professional footballer into the action that allowed me to manifest the dream and vision. There is no doubt that excitement and determination sparked the motion, against all odds, to do what was required to become a successful author. As I write this book, I am still heavily focused on promoting my seventh book, *The Wellness Puzzle*, and creating a wave of wellness worldwide. I am disturbed by the sickness rate, both physical, mental, and emotional, across the world. I am totally agitated into motion to engage the un-engageable, move the un-moveable and motivate those who cannot be motivated. I want to help people move towards making better choices, and living the life of health, happiness, and abundance they are born and destined to live.

Emotion will move us in a direction. The direction it takes us, and the result of that direction, is dependent on the nature of the emotion experienced because of the thoughts we choose to focus on. The sad reality is we seem conditioned to think the worst, and human nature generally seems to take us down a thought path that leads us to an undesirable consequence. This tendency towards worry, anxiety, and stress seems to be hard-wired into our very being. That being the case, we need to work extra hard to create new conditioning.

Suppose we constantly focus on and are driven by fear, anxiety, anger, resentment, worry or bitterness. In that case, it won't end well for many reasons. Firstly, as I've already touched on and will expand in later chapters, emotion drives our actions towards joy, happiness, achievement, fulfilment, pain, suffering, devastation, and regret. I know which of these I want, and I'm confident I know what you want, so be very careful of your thought choices.

As I have mentioned, my mission is to create a worldwide wave of wellness, and for people to live a life of joyful longevity. I am very aware of the impact of our emotional state on our physical health and well-being. Obviously, the actions we take due to our emotions will impact habits that will affect physical and mental health. But even more significant than that is the immediate chemical, hormonal, and physiological impact of emotions, both positive and negative, on the body.

As I write this chapter, my father's partner, Annette, has recently celebrated her mother's 100th birthday. My dad and Annette came to my house for lunch the week before the birthday, and we were discussing her mother's longevity. Annette explained how her mother had the remarkable ability to let go of stressful things, not worry, and find positive in all situations. This, my friend, is an example of the powerful impact of our emotional state on our physical well-being. It is now backed up by research and science as the key to living a long and happy life.

In Chapter 2, I mentioned the paragraph from a book called *The Magic is in the Extra Mile* by Larry Di Angi, and how it talked about the keys to joyful longevity. I discussed many of the physical impacts of emotion on the body in my book, *The Wellness Puzzle*. However, I feel it's worth discussing in more detail here. I will touch on five main areas of impact that significantly affect lives, both good and bad, due to our emotional state. They are the immune system, DNA, brain health, free-radical activity, and cortisol.

Immune System

I think we would all agree a strong and fortified immune system is vital for a long, happy, and healthy life. There are now many studies showing the impact of emotion on our immune system. One study I read suggested only five minutes of feeling anger, resentment, bitterness, anxiety or similar, can shut down the immune system for as long as five or six hours. Yes, I said <u>shut down</u>! That means to switch off, disengage, disable, and render inoperable. This means our bodies are vulnerable to attacks from germs, viruses, and toxins.

I found this next piece of information at www.newscientist.com:

> In 2003, Richard Davidson of the University of Wisconsin in the USA led a team that studied the effect of emotion on the pre-frontal cortex (PFC) of the brain. People who had the greatest activity in the right PFC when asked to dwell on distressing episodes in their life had a markedly lower antibody level after influenza vaccination. In contrast, those showing exceptional activity in the left PFC when recalling happy times developed high antibody levels.

> With colleagues at Wisconsin and Princeton University, New Jersey, Davidson asked 52 men and women who graduated from Wisconsin in 1957 to recount both the

best and worst events in their lives on paper. For their best experiences, the subjects were asked to write about an event where they experienced *intense happiness or joy*. And for their worst experience, they were asked to remember an event causing *the most intense sadness, fear, or anger.*

During this autobiographical task, the electrical activity of the brain was measured. The subjects were then given flu shots, and their antibody levels were measured after two weeks, four weeks and six months. The researcher found a clear link between strong activity in the left PFC and a large rise in antibodies, and vice versa. However, the study could not explain exactly how having a positive attitude boosts the immune system. The researchers say some evidence exists to suggest a link between the PFC and the immune system via a complex hormonal system governed by the hypothalamus, pituitary, and adrenal glands.

As you can see, the researchers could not explain why positive emotion is better for the immune system than negative. However, do we really need science? I know I don't. If feeling great will increase my antibodies and strengthen my immune system, I will focus on positive thoughts and emotions. What about you?

DNA

So, what about DNA? It has long been thought that our DNA is fixed, can't be changed, and it's either good luck or bad luck. I have a friend, Peter, who is in his late fifties, and based on his genetics and DNA, should not be alive today. Peter has an *impressive* family history, as he describes it. His dad died at age fifty from a heart attack. His brother died at age 45 from a heart attack after having a stroke at forty. His mother died after a stroke at age 71. He has two sisters and a brother who all have high blood pressure, high cholesterol and weight issues and have had double heart bypass surgery. All his siblings are taking medications. His aunt has a sixty per cent blockage in her carotid artery. His uncle has a 99 per cent blockage in his carotid artery. His grandparents all passed away with diabetes, high blood pressure and high cholesterol. Whoa! I'm feeling exhausted just listing these people and their conditions!

Incredibly, Peter is healthy, happy, lean, and continually baffling his cardiologist. How is this possible? I'll return to Peter shortly, but now I want to take some well-researched ideas from www.powerofpositivity. com. In an article on this website, Dr Dave Woynarowksi explains growing evidence that stressful thoughts and emotions shorten lifespan, which researchers can measure through DNA changes.

> At the 2011 *Longevity Now Conference*, Dr Woynarowksi spoke about telomeres, the parts of DNA like a biological time clock determining how much time a person have left to live. Telomeres are responsible for every cellular mechanism. We can live longer and slow down the ageing process by doing two things:
>
> 1. slow down the loss of telomeres; and
> 2. add length to the telomeres.
>
> Researchers believe that telomere length is potentially a metaphor for the length of your life. The longer the telomeres, the longer we have left to live. Telomeres are stretches of DNA that cap our chromosomes and help

prevent chromosomal deterioration. Shortened telomeres aren't known to cause a specific disease *per se* and are shorter in people with cancer, diabetes, heart disease and high stress levels. We want our telomeres intact.

Mindfulness and meditation are two ways to use thoughts to help keep telomeres intact. A study of breast cancer patients and telomere length found those who practised mindfulness meditation could keep their telomeres longer. You will find this study on the Internet, https://www.ncbi.nlm.nih.gov/pmc/articles/PMC2719778/. At the same time, the control group who did not meditate had shortened the telomere end of their DNA.

The researchers believe supportive conversations that enable emotional expression are also helpful. Whether you talk to your friends, relatives, or a therapist, expressing your emotions is a way to change your thinking about a situation. By discussing problems, we can often see a solution is available by changing our mindset.

While being mindful helps keep your DNA telomeres long, the opposite is also true in that telomeres are shortened by stress. Researchers looked at DNA telomere length and stress levels in another research study on DNA and negative thoughts.

The scientists found that *women with the highest levels of perceived stress have telomeres shorter on average by the equivalent of at least one decade of additional ageing than low-stress women. These findings have implications for understanding how, at the cellular level, stress may promote the early onset of age-related diseases.*

Women who had more stress had shorter life spans as measured by their DNA. For those concerned about their well-being and health, these research results are enough to make you seek out ways to change your thoughts and have a positive impact on your DNA.

This seems to support evidence as to how my Annette's mother lived to 100 and beyond. Okay, let's get back to my friend Peter. Several years ago, his wife suggested he go to one of Australia's leading Interventional cardiologists to get checked. Deep down, Peter knew he was fine, but he did it to keep peace and harmony in the house. To all men reading this, that's a good lesson. Peter explained his family history to the cardiologist. Without any further examination, this medical professional suggested Peter immediately starts a course of aspirin to thin his blood. Peter said *no* and asked the doctor to do some simple non-invasive tests.

The cardiologist complied and was astounded to discover how healthy Peter really was. The reason is simple. For many years, Peter, knowing about his family history and not wanting it to determine his life, has focused on his thinking and emotional state. He was, and is, heavily involved in positive personal development, associates with supportive and encouraging people to meditate daily, and is a happy and purpose-driven man. He makes great choices with his eating and exercise, and consequently, his telomeres are long and healthy.

Brain Health

I think we would all agree, our brain is an important part of our body. In fact, it is the most miraculous piece of divine engineering ever. Wow, the capacity of what the brain can do is incredible and way beyond what most people can, or will, ever comprehend in their lifetime. We want a healthy brain, right? That would have to be the understatement of the century. If how we use our brain determines the thoughts we create, and those thoughts lead us to an emotional state, we use our brain to either strengthen or destroy itself.

Someone who inspires, educates, and sometimes confuses me a little, is Dr Caroline Leaf. The bio on her website reads:

> *Dr Caroline Leaf is a cognitive neuroscientist with a PhD in Communication Pathology and a BSc in Logopedics and Audiology, specialising in metacognitive and cognitive neuropsychology. Since the early 1980s, she has studied and researched the Mind-Brain connection and did some of the initial research back in the late 80s showing the neuroplasticity of the brain. During her years in clinical practice and her work with thousands of underprivileged teachers and students in South Africa and the USA as a communication pathologist and cognitive neuroscientist, she developed an original theory of the science of thought and tools and processes based on this research. This real-world neuroscience research, Dr Leaf did back then, becoming popular now as a research tool, helps people develop and change their thinking and subsequent behaviour. Her science of thought technique has transformed the lives of patients with Traumatic Brain Injury (TBI), chronic traumatic encephalopathy (CTE), learning disabilities (ADD, ADHD),*

autism, dementia, emotional traumas, and mental health issues. It has shown thousands of students of all ages, and adults and corporations how to use their minds to detox and develop their brains.

So yes, Dr Leaf knows stuff. I just want to take one simple quote from a blog on her website dated 31 July 2019. It says,

If you let your toxic emotions grow unchecked by thinking about them and ruminating on your feelings, you will feel worse because the resultant neurochemical chaos can cause brain damage and dramatically affect your mental and physical well-being.

Do you know what? That's good enough for me!

Toxins and Free Radical Activity

Mental and emotional stress, anxiety, anger, and other similar emotions, if not controlled, can be incredibly toxic to the body. As I have already described and done so in more detail in *The Wellness Puzzle,* toxins are not good for your physical health. Whilst you may be deliberately doing all the right things to purify and detoxify, toxins are still infiltrating from all angles. Your body is also working away twenty-four-seven to destroy and keep any remaining toxins at bay. Inside your cells, chemical reactions are continually happening to remove and eliminate toxins. The unfortunate by-products of these chemical reactions are nasty tiny atoms called **free radicals.**

I'm going to keep this as simple as possible. My aim here is not for you to have a complete physiological and scientific understanding. It is for you to be aware of the devastating impact of free radicals and commit to positive action. I hope you're okay with that.

From the moment there is any stress on, and toxicity in, the body, chemical reactions are happening to eliminate toxins. As I mentioned earlier, the by-products of these chemical reactions are free radicals. These by-products are unstable atoms missing an electron that react quickly with any other compounds to capture the needed electron and regain stability. When the attacked compound loses an electron, it becomes a free radical itself, and a chain reaction of damage begins. Once this process begins, it quickly escalates and results in the disruption of a living cell.

Some free radicals are produced normally during metabolism and are a part of the body's process to help neutralise viruses and bacteria. The body should be able to handle the normal free radical activity. However, we live in crazy times. We are continually subjected to chronic stress and our propensity to negative thoughts and emotions. In addition, the fact we are not eating enough of the nutrients that neutralise free radicals, means they have become a seriously devastating problem.

Various studies and theories have connected oxidative stress from free radicals to:

- Central nervous system diseases, such as Alzheimer's and other dementias.
- Cardiovascular disease due to clogged arteries.
- Autoimmune and inflammatory disorders, such as rheumatoid arthritis and cancer.
- Cataracts and age-related vision decline.
- Age-related changes in appearance, such as loss of skin elasticity, wrinkles, greying hair, hair loss, and changes in hair texture.
- Diabetes.

- Genetic degenerative diseases, such as Huntington's disease or Parkinson's.

One of the simplest things we can do to minimise and reverse the devastating damage of free radicals is to change the thoughts that lead to our emotional response.

Cortisol

Imagine back in prehistoric times when life was much simpler. Amongst the cave people community, there was a man named Ugg and his woman Igg. Ugg loved Igg and would take her with him everywhere he went, dragging her along the ground by her hair! Life was great as they lived simply and enjoyed everything that nature had to offer. They enjoyed the sun, open spaces, fresh food, pure air, and clean water. There were only the occasional challenges. Those rare instances when Ugg had to avoid the clutches of the devilish Tyrannosaurus rex (T-Rex).

One day, Ugg strolled out of his cave to do some berry picking. A few minutes later, he heard a terrifying unmistakable sound behind him. It was the nasal snorting of T-Rex. He turned slowly, heart racing, to see those fearsome eyes staring straight at him, and a hungry T-Rex drooling over his next meal. Ugg had other plans. He felt the hormones and emotions build in his body. He felt himself growing a bit taller as he prepared himself for drastic action.

He looked at T-Rex, screamed at the top of his lungs and turned and ran in the opposite direction as fast as he could. From somewhere within, he found the speed and agility he didn't know he had, as he darted in and around trees, over hills, and through caves, with T-Rex hungry and hot on his tail. There were a few close calls, and T-Rex almost had his dinner, but somehow Ugg had evaded the beast, found his way back to his cave, slammed the rock door behind and collapsed at the feet of

Igg. He was safe at last! Ugg spent the next thirty minutes recovering, allowing his heart rate to return to normal and enjoying it as his fear and anxiety melted away.

What was it that saved Ugg from the T-Rex? Amongst other things, it was cortisol. Cortisol is a steroid hormone produced by the adrenal glands and is released when there is any stress on, or perceived threat to, the body. It's a *fight or flight* hormone. It worked beautifully for me in my days as a professional footballer. Any time an angry opposition player was heading for me, I was very grateful for cortisol! I used to joke – even though I wasn't joking when I said it – I won all my fights by fifty metres!

In Ugg's case, when he was aware of T-Rex and his imminent danger, his fear activated his adrenal glands, which responded by releasing cortisol into the bloodstream. The result was that his blood sugar levels raised, and his blood pressure increased in preparation for him to stand and fight or to turn and run. It was a good thing for Ugg he took the latter option! It gave him speed, strength, and agility he didn't know he had, and it enabled him to escape the clutches of the fierce beast and get safely back to his cave. After a short time, his body stopped producing cortisol. His blood sugar and blood pressure levels returned to normal, and all was good. Ugg and Igg just had to eat leftovers that night because Ugg was unable to collect any fresh berries!

As you see from this 'factual' story, cortisol is a good thing and is necessary for all of us at times in our life. When stress and danger are occasional things, cortisol is useful and a very important bodily function. Let's fast forward the tape, however, from the prehistoric age to today. Is stress an occasional thing, or is it a chronic and ongoing issue? I think you know the answer to that.

Many people spend much of their lives stressed, anxious, rushing, fearful, and in many other negative emotional states. This means that the body is over-producing cortisol. Can you imagine, or have experienced, the impact of increased blood sugar levels and blood pressure?

According to Dr Lissa Rankin, MD, there are signs and symptoms that cortisol is being over-produced in your body. This includes affected sleep, fatigue (even with good sleep), weight gain (specially around the abdomen, even when you eat well and exercise), and increased susceptibility to colds and other infections. In addition, there may be unhealthy cravings, a propensity for backaches and headaches, diminished sex drive, gut issues, anxiety, and mood swings.

Yikes! Cortisol is causing many undesirable physical issues. Isn't it comforting to know most of these issues can be alleviated if the cause of cortisol is removed? Well, my friend, in most cases, you hold the key to doing just that in your hands. When you realise you get to choose where you focus your thoughts, you can change the stress, anxiety, fear, anger, resentment, and other similar emotions. Simply choose to focus on thoughts that will lead to gratitude, love, empathy, and empowerment.

Emotion is your body's way of talking to you. Are you listening?

Despite everything I have said about the healthy and unhealthy impact of emotion on our actions, outcomes and physical well-being, all emotion is good. Now, this may sound like a total contradiction. However, it's only the emotion we hold in our body that will have a long-term impact. We just need to know which ones to hold on to and which ones to let go of, just like Annette's 100-year-old mother, who learned how to hold onto joy and let go of stress and worry.

The feelings we experience are, in fact, simply our body's way of telling us how we are thinking, how we are looking at something, or what we are believing. So, in a lot of ways, our emotional state is actually a very useful way of helping us move forward in our lives if we choose to pay attention to it. Yes, that's the key phrase here, so let me repeat it and bold it for emphasis: **if we choose to pay attention to it**.

Emotion is your body's way of saying: *'Hello! I am here, and I have some vital information for you that will enhance your life. You just need to listen to me and take the appropriate action.'* As it was for me, the issue may be that certain emotional states are so chronic you no longer pay attention to them. You may have just learned to live with them. If those emotional states are gratitude, love, joy, empathy, forgiveness, empowerment, excitement, and happiness, let them be. If, however, they have a different and not as healthy orientation, then please, for your sake, listen and act.

I truly believe all emotions are valuable. They are communicating vital information to you. When you feel grateful, it means you are focusing on the right stuff. When you feel forgiveness, you are focusing on healing. When you feel empathy, you are focusing on the welfare of others. When you feel joy, you are focusing on what you love. When you feel love, you are focusing on what makes your heart sing. When you feel empowered, you are focusing on what you can do. When you feel the excitement, you are focusing on what you want to do. These are incredibly positive and healthy ways to focus our thoughts.

Now, let's look at the flip side and the emotions many people consider negative or bad. When you feel anger, it means something has happened that has conflicted with your values. When you feel fear, it means you are focused on what you are unsure you can handle. When you are anxious, you are focused on what you don't want. When you are resentful, you are holding on to something that it's maybe time to let go of and forgive. When you are bitter, you have held on for too long, and it's time to let go. When you are depressed, you can't see a way forward. When you are overwhelmed, you are focused on too many things at once.

Can you see how valuable this information is? Well, it's only valuable if you take notice of it and act on it. Staying in these emotional states means staying focused on the stuff you don't like and don't want. This will lead to poorly considered choices and undesirable outcomes. As you now know, it will also allow these emotions to stay in the body and is very damaging to your physical well-being. In the next chapter, I will outline how to see and use ALL emotions to move forward in life. Just know, your life is ruled by the emotional states you allow to be persistent.

Moving towards 'TEARS of Joy'

> Proverbs 17:22 – *A joyful heart is good medicine, but a broken spirit dries up the bones.* (NASB)

I believe this scripture. I have observed this, and I want to emphasise this to you. It's not only our health and well-being impacted by our spirit, our heart, or our emotional state, but it's everything important to us.

Our greatest strength, and the biggest challenge, is that we are human beings, and emotional beings at that. It's what sets us apart from animals. It is what can move us to some of the most miraculous achievements, incredible joy, and wonderful longevity, or it can take us down to the pit of despair and tragedy. All of this depends on the emotional state we choose to stay in, based on the thoughts we focus on, what we believe, and how we perceive circumstances.

I love being emotional. In fact, I'm emotional about being emotional! I love feeling joy, gratitude, adoration, accomplishment, pride, and empowerment. There are even times when I enjoy feeling some of what we consider negative emotions – like sadness, fear, and melancholy. It makes us who we are and separates us from animals. A controlled amount of the whole spectrum of human emotion can help us perform at a higher level, care more, and become better. We just need to make sure we don't stay in a potentially destructive or unhealthy emotional state for too long.

In this chapter, I really want to get across that everything you do, say, and end up with, results from an emotionally driven action or re-action. Whether this is conscious or not, it started with a thought you chose to focus on. Your emotions drive actions that lead to habits, and your emotions cause chemical, physical, and physiological changes in your body. Your emotional state can take you up to a life of optimal well-being and purpose-driven happiness. The alternative is to drag you down to experience poor health and devastating occurrences in your life. Choose carefully and, in the next chapter, we will explore how to use your emotions for good, not evil!

Key questions and action steps

1. When you think of your emotional state, for the most part, and based on what you now know, would you say it's mostly helping you move forward in your life, or is it holding you back?
2. If you are unsure how to answer the first question, are you happy with the results you are currently getting in all areas of your life? That's a good place to start.
3. Can you see a correlation between those results and your predominant emotional states?
4. Is it an area you feel you can improve on?
5. Start today to listen to your body and emotions to tell you what's happening. The more awareness you have, the more you can use all emotions to help you in your life.
6. Would you like to know how to take control and use your powerful emotions to lead you in a happy, healthy, purposeful, and successful direction? If yes, please keep reading.

CHAPTER 9

Developing emotional intelligence

"The key to emotional intelligence is all about the willingness to believe that you are enough."

This is possibly the most important chapter in the book, and the hardest to write. Why hard to write? Because I am writing this as much for me as I am for you. I am still very much a work in progress when it comes to emotional intelligence. So, what is it? After doing some research on Google, I found a definition that states:

> Emotional intelligence *is the capacity to be aware of, control, and express one's emotions and handle interpersonal relationships judiciously and empathetically.*

In brackets after this definition, it also says: *'emotional intelligence is the key to both personal and professional success'.* Why would that be the case? What about IQ and intellect? What about talent and natural ability? What about position, background, education, family history, opportunities, luck, and all the other things people suggest are critical factors required for personal and professional success? This is big. This is not what most people know or believe. This could be a life-changing revelation for you, as it was for me.

One of the many books I have read, and been impacted by, is *Grit* by Angela Duckworth. The subtitle of the book is '*The Power of Passion and Perseverance*'. It isn't '*The Power of Intellect and IQ*'. It isn't '*The Power of Talent and Natural Ability*'. It isn't '*The Power of Luck and Being in the Right Place at the Right Time*'. The power of passion and perseverance is available to every single person on the planet. It is just a decision and a willingness to be aware of and manage our emotional state.

In the book, Angela talks about the concept that *effort counts twice*. To formalise achievement, she splits it into two simple formulas to determine one's skill level and ability to achieve great things. Formula one: ***Skill = Talent x Effort***. Formula two: ***Achievement = Skill x Effort***. It is interesting to note from these formulas that skill and achievement have far less to do with talent, intellect, and natural ability, and much more to do with effort. Effort is simply determined and focused action. This is because the emotional drive to achieve something far outweighs the logic, which suggests it can't be done, or is too hard, because of the many *logical* factors that will sway most people.

I inadvertently applied these two equations to turn limited ability into a seven-year professional sporting career and a passionate life as a best-selling author. Let me show you a simple example that illustrates why emotional intelligence, not intellect or natural ability, is the key to a successful, happy, and abundant life. Let's look at two fictitious people, John and Mary. They don't know each other and are starting at the same time working to achieve the same outcome, yet they are two very different people.

John is very talented and naturally gifted in this hypothetical area, so he scores a 3 out of 3 for talent. Unfortunately for him, and because of his natural ability, John doesn't think he needs to work as hard and gets easily discouraged, so his effort is minimal. He scores only a 1 out of 3. His skill level is calculated by multiplying talent by effort: 3 x 1 = 3. So, he has a skill score of 3. On the other hand, Mary has a minimal natural ability in this same area. So, from a young age, she has learned that to achieve anything she wants, she needs to work harder than most. She has a talent score of 1 out of 3 and an effort score of 3 out of 3. Therefore, her skill is 1 x 3 = 3. Isn't it interesting that, even though John has three times more talent, their skill level is the same?

If they have the same skill level, you may think their achievement would also be similar. Not so, because effort counts twice. John has a skill of 3 but an effort of only 1, so his overall achievement score is 3 x 1 = 3. This is where the less talented Mary shines. She is not upset that she has less natural ability. She has come to terms with it, so she is more determined than ever. With a skill of 3 and an effort of 3, her achievement ends up as 3 x 3 = 9. Wow! Mary has one-third of the talent but ends up with three times the achievement because her focus is on effort. This is evidence of a very high level of emotional intelligence.

Can you imagine what would happen if John combined his natural talent with the effort that comes through emotional intelligence? Let's do some more sums. If his effort score was 3, and his talent score was 3, his skill score would be 9. With a skill of 9, and his newly acquired effort of 3, his achievement score is now 27. Can you see the amazing exponential power that comes with emotionally intelligent effort, irrespective of other circumstances?

I am a *Mary* of the world. As I have mentioned, I don't have much natural ability, but I have a strong work ethic and application of effort. As a teenager, during my time at the St Kilda Football Club, I didn't understand the concept of emotional intelligence. It was just what I did. I was often confused because, at the start of each football season, a new batch of aspiring footballers would come through and try out at the club.

Many of them had far more natural ability than I did. I would look at them at training, be dazzled by their skills, and be certain that my days were numbered. Miraculously, year after year, I would stay, and many of them would go. In my mind, I couldn't work it out. Until the year, Colin came along.

Colin was one man who intrigued me (I have changed his name to protect his identity). I don't think I had met or played with anyone with more natural ability than this guy. It was almost like he had the ball on a string. He was agile, balanced, poised and in control. He could mark well, handball brilliantly and kick the ball long and accurately with both feet. He was technically brilliant.

It didn't take me long to work out that he wasn't going to last long either. His attitude was atrocious and emotional intelligence was barely existent! He would never push himself to the limit at training. He would complain when the weather wasn't perfect. It was always too hot, too cold, too wet, or too windy! When a tough part of the training was coming up, he would consistently and conveniently suffer an injury. That recurring hamstring injury would happen to pop up just at the right time. So, while his teammates were slogging it out on the training track in searing heat or freezing cold, he would retire to the medical room for a relaxing massage and treatment.

Before the season started and the final list for the season was read out, he couldn't understand why he wasn't on it. He then went into victim mode. *They didn't like me. They didn't help me enough. They have no idea what true talent really is. It's a terrible club. I'm glad. I don't want to be here anyway.* It was everyone's fault but his, and he just couldn't see that it had nothing to do with his talent but everything to do with his atrocious attitude and lack of effort.

So, how do we develop emotional intelligence? This is the ten-million-dollar question, right? At the risk of losing you right here, the first thing I need to tell you is that it is not easy, and there is no quick-fix solution. If you go to some doctors, they may prescribe a pill you can take, but certainly not one that will give a long-term solution without side effects. It will take focus, and it will take deliberate attention over an extended period to create a permanent change in your thinking and behaviours.

There are a few simple strategies that have made a difference in my life and helped me become a much more emotionally intelligent person. Please don't get me wrong, I am still very much a work in progress, and have a long way to go, but I am aware and working on it. As I mentioned, there is no easy solution, and there is no perfect strategy. The key will be to pick one or two strategies and stick at them, even if you feel like they are taking too long or not working. This will be your first test on whether you can develop the emotional intelligence that will transform your life.

I am enough

The greatest barrier to success, happiness, health, wealth, and any type of abundance is the deep-down feeling most of us have, that *we aren't enough*. Through a range of messages, feedback, and opinions we have received over the course of our life, from different people and experiences, we have come to believe we are not smart enough, good-looking enough, sexy enough, strong enough, worthy enough, or deserving enough. We just do not feel good enough. This belief is a lie, and it's destroying lives all around the world.

Marissa Peer is a best-selling author, motivational speaker and leading celebrity therapist and pioneering hypnotherapist trainer. On her website, www.marissapeer.com, she has this to say:

> It's such a thrill when I get to hear how people I've never even met manage to improve their lives by using my techniques and advice. Last week served as a

good example. I was giving a talk to a group of female entrepreneurs and business leaders about simple steps they can use to mastermind their lives and feel confident in their relationships and careers. At the conclusion of my talk, a woman in the audience raised her hand and said that, for the past few months, she's set a reminder on her phone at 8:00 am and 8:00 pm every day. It says simply: "*I am enough.*"

This is a trick I have encouraged my clients to use for years. The repetition of that simple phrase over and over (both out loud and in your head) will eventually make it difficult for your mind to object to it. As the audience member said, even though she didn't feel rich enough, smart enough, thin enough, or successful enough when she first programmed the words into her phone, she slowly but surely began to believe the powerful message itself.

In my 25 years as a therapist, I've discovered that the root of so many modern problems – hoarding, excessive drinking, compulsive shopping, and over-eating – come right back to a need to fill the inner emptiness of not feeling *enough* with external things. The more you tell yourself you are enough, the more you'll believe it. It sounds so utterly simple – and it is – and all you need is the commitment to do it and the belief that it will work.

I couldn't have said it any better than Marissa. If you have any negative feelings stemming from a belief that you aren't enough in any area of your life, you need to deal with it, or it will take you down, time and time again. Go to Marissa's website and learn about her work. It is truly life changing.

Capture emotion

The biggest issue for many people is they don't realise or acknowledge they control their emotional state. It is far too easy to blame other people, situations, and circumstances for being angry, sad, bitter, resentful, fearful, anxious, or unhappy. As you now know, your emotional state results from a thought or thoughts you chose to pay attention to and hang on to. If you can choose thoughts that lead to these disempowering emotions, then you can change them. All you need to do is to choose ones that will lead to powerful and encouraging emotions. You do this by capturing emotions, validating them, identifying the thought that initiated the feeling and, if required, changing the thought, belief, or perspective. Yes, it is that simple. It is just not easy.

At the end of the last chapter, I mentioned all emotions are valuable. Emotions are how our body talks to us and tells us what's happening, and whether we need to change focus, create new beliefs, look for another perspective, or not. The question is, are we listening and paying attention? While it will take some time, patience, and focus, you can teach yourself this wonderful awareness strategy. If you do, it will have an immediate and incredible impact on all areas of your life.

What do I mean by capturing emotion? I mean, become aware of it, acknowledge it, bring it to the light, validate and normalise it – because we are emotional human beings, and all emotion is valuable, right? Once we have done this, we can deal with it, if necessary, rather than react to it or stuff it down and try to ignore it, hide it, or cover it. The very moment you push down a disempowering and potentially unhealthy emotion and try to avoid it, you set off a ticking time bomb. At some stage in the future, this ticking time bomb will explode, leaving devastation and rubble. You know what I mean here, don't you? You have experienced this before in your life, haven't you? The truth is, we all have.

On the flip side, when you can capture a powerfully encouraging, inquisitive or questioning emotion, identify it, and understand what your thoughts leading to it are. Then you can learn how to be in that positive, evolving, growing and happy place more often. This strategy of capturing emotion works beautifully for the entire spectrum of human emotion.

For me, the emotion of anxiety has been a consistent part of my life for many years. I would often wake up with an underlying feeling of anxiety. I didn't know where it was coming from for most of my life or why it was there, so I just stuffed it down, ignored it, and got on with my day. I couldn't understand why undesirable things were continually happening in my life until I started to acknowledge and question this anxiety. I remember the day when I woke up, sick of the feeling and the results I was getting in my life.

For the first time, I became very aware of the anxiety and validated it. I visualised holding the anxiety in my hands, bringing up to the light, acknowledging it, and asking myself, *I am feeling anxiety here. There must be a reason. Why am I feeling this emotion?*

At the time, I really couldn't answer the question. The feeling had been with me for so long, and the thoughts leading to it were so deeply buried in my unconscious mind, that I had to really take time to reflect and get the truth. Over a period of time, and by continually capturing the emotion, the answer came to me. My deep-down belief was that I wasn't good enough. No matter what was happening in my life, the voice in my head was telling me I was not smart enough, talented enough or good enough. This is why I was chasing external validation.

I decided that needed to change, and so I got on board with Marissa Peer's strategy. I started telling myself, reminding myself, and believing I am good enough, and boy did things change! The reality is we all have deep-down unconscious beliefs that are causing emotional responses we often can't explain. So following the same process I adopted is a good idea. What about all those regular one-off circumstances that lead us to anger, sadness, resentment, guilt, shame, frustration, or fear on a daily basis?

If you can get into the routine of capturing every emotion, bringing it to the light, validating it, changing the thought (if required), your life will change forever. Trust me on this one. Have notes and reminders around until it becomes second nature to you. Then the moment you feel an emotion that may become an unhealthy one, start taking hold and pounce into action. You will never eliminate emotion from your life, nor do you want to. Not all those seemingly unhealthy emotions are bad. However, I encourage you to get good at dealing with damaging emotion swiftly, and entirely, as soon as it starts talking to you.

Like you, I am tapped on the shoulder or slapped in the face (as the case may be) by potentially dangerous emotions every single day. Despite that, thankfully, I am calm, relaxed, and peaceful these days, as I have learned how to listen to, capture, validate, and deal with all emotions! I have, however, been prone, in my past, to let a little road rage slip into my normally calm demeanour. This would happen if someone cut me off, was driving too slowly, pulled in front of me and braked, or pushed in front of me trying to queue hop which, by the way, I did all the time. I would get angry, sit on my horn, and even tell them about it. Well, just the other day I was in the car and a few of those things happened, one after another. I was on the freeway, and some crazy speeding and lane-hopping car cut in front of me as it flew past. Soon after, on the same freeway, someone came alongside me, moved past me, changed into my lane just in front of me, and then slowed down, causing me to hit the brakes. Then, five minutes later, as I was in the left lane waiting to turn, someone pushed their way in front of me to jump the queue.

I could feel the anger brewing. I quickly captured that anger, and it wasn't hard to identify the thought that led to it. I won't repeat it here, as I don't want to offend anyone. I was quick to change my thought to gratitude. I am in control, am a good driver, and can easily negotiate the traffic and other drivers. The anger magically disappeared, I was left calm and peaceful, and I continued to drive with control and good sense.

Developing the awareness, persistence, and habit of capturing all emotions, bringing each to the light, identifying the thoughts, validating them, and changing them is an invaluable part of creating emotional intelligence.

Faith

Faith, again? Yes, indeed. I strongly feel it belongs here and is an important part of developing emotional intelligence. I am talking about the word, the concept, its meaning, and the impact it will have if applied in your life. You see, the word is a powerful one and will totally change your whole deal if you embrace it. The Google definition of the word faith is *'complete trust or confidence in someone or something'*. The keywords in that definition are *'complete trust'*. Not *some trust,* or *trust if,* but *complete trust.*

I have already spoken about my incredible life-changing faith journey with Christianity so far. I can say, with no doubt in my mind, my favourite passage in the Bible is the one about faith. As mentioned, Hebrews 11:1 says *'Faith is the substance of things hoped for, the evidence of things not seen'*. If that is a little hard to get your head around then, as you know, author Phillip Yancey describes faith this way: '*faith means trusting in advance what will only make sense in reverse'*. What both of those definitions, descriptions, quotes, or whatever you want to call them are saying is that you don't need to worry!

The most potentially dangerous of all the emotions are stress, worry, and anxiety. I do consider them to be dangerous if we don't address them. We live in a day and age with many situations that lead people to live with chronic stress, worry, and anxiety. So, in my mind, the greatest antidote if these three emotions become an issue, is faith.

If we look at Phillip Yancey's definition, it totally describes my life to this point. If you are reading this, it's my eighth published book. I am living a life I love, doing meaningful things with the people I care about most. To be honest, every day, I think about, and are grateful for, this wonderful life. I pinch myself to make sure I am awake. I continually ask myself: *how did I get here?* If you asked me twenty years ago if this would be the life I want to be living, I would have said *YES. That would be incredible, and I would love to, but I have no idea how that could possibly happen.*

At that starting point, looking in advance, it was not logical, made no sense, and didn't even really seem possible. The thought was overwhelming and stressful. However, looking back from where I am today, I can see the logical steps that led me to this point in my life. I can see how my football career shaped much of my thinking and attitudes. I can see why getting sacked from St Kilda Football Club was actually a great thing, and opened the door for my wellness industry career. I can see how moving from gym to gym and finally landing in personal training fuelled my passion for making a difference. I can see how, and why, I decided to buy a café, and how the failure of said café led to the illogical decision to write my first book. I know the rest of the events unfolded as they were meant to unfold to get me here today. It all makes sense, in reverse.

If I had known then what I know now, I would have been more peaceful and certain through the many uncertain and traumatic years. I can't go back to the me of twenty years ago and give myself that information. However, I can move forward from today with faith and peace, knowing that everything will fall into place, just as it is meant to. I have total faith in God and that everything is taken care of in my life to help me live my destiny and purpose. It is the most peaceful and healthy feeling I have ever experienced.

With all my heart, I want to encourage you to explore this powerful yet misunderstood concept. In my book *The Wellness Puzzle,* it is one of the seven pieces of the puzzle leading to a life of joyful longevity. Why? Because, through its very definition, it brings peace, confidence, calmness, certainty, and all the emotions that will lead you to health, happiness, longevity, and success. The best news is that faith is not an ability you need to acquire, not a book you need to read, and not a character trait you need to develop. Faith is a choice and one that you can make right now.

In September 2019, I spent the entire month in the USA launching my book, *The Wellness Puzzle,* and spreading my message. In a talk with carers in a Missouri hospice, I discussed the idea of joyful longevity and the power of our emotional state on the length and quality of life. One of the carers in the audience shared about a lady he worked with who lived joyfully to 113 years old. He could never understand how she lived so long, based on her lifestyle habits. She smoked, she drank alcohol and, every day, she ate deep-fried, fatty, and sugary foods. One day he asked her: "I don't understand how you do it. How do you live so well and for so long, smoking, drinking and eating the way you do?"

Are you ready for the answer? It's mind-blowing. She said: "Simple. I don't worry about anything. I trust in God and have faith that he will look after me." Yes, this is an isolated example. Yes, there may be other reasons why this lady was miraculously able to live so well and for so long. Yes, there may not be any hard scientific data to back this up. However, if having faith is, and was, the reason, then I'm not going to take any chances. I'm going to have faith. What about you?

As you begin exploring this idea, and I hope you do, you will discover many different types and platforms of faith. Find the one which works for you and stick with it. I am Christian, and my faith in God has made an amazing difference in my life in many ways. You can have faith in God, in the Universe, in your ability, in karma, that everything will be okay, there is good in everything, and everything happens for a reason. My strongest encouragement to you, if creating emotional intelligence is a priority, don't miss the power of faith to help you on the journey.

An attitude independent of circumstances

Everything I have spoken about will help develop an attitude independent of circumstances. It will take time and practice but, once achieved, it is the point at which you have created emotional intelligence. It is the culmination of all the other things I have just spoken about. So what does it mean? It means your emotional state is not dependent on what's happening to you at that time. In other words, you don't let your mood be dictated by the events in your life. Just because something seemingly bad happens doesn't mean you have to be sad, resentful, angry, or bitter. You can choose a different response.

To really emphasise the power of this attitude choice, I want to tell the story of a lady who lost more than one million dollars in about thirty seconds. I was listening to this story on audio a few years ago. It really resonated with me how one small lapse in emotional intelligence can have a devastating long-term impact. The story is narrated by a man who witnessed the whole event and saw it from an independent and unbiased observer's perspective.

Early one morning, he was driving in his car, heading to the gym in his country hometown, when he noticed a car speed past him. The car was being driven by a local real estate agent. He knew this because the car had her name, picture, and job title all over it. Just as the speeding car had overtaken the narrator, an old run-down pick-up truck turned onto the main road, seemingly not seeing her, and cut in front of her. She slammed on the brakes and skidded to miss him and came to a stop, luckily without making contact or causing damage to either car. As the man telling the story described it, he could see things flying around inside the realtor's car. She wound down her window and started using some very colourful language directed at the pick-up truck driver, who was blissfully unaware that any of this was happening.

The lady drove off and soon parked at a local convenience store. The man who was narrating thought this would make a good story, so he followed her. She got out of the car and was wearing a beautiful cream outfit. Unfortunately, it now had coffee stains all over it because, in the near collision, she spilt the coffee she was drinking all over herself. She was obviously angry, and stormed into the convenience store, found the restroom to try and clean herself up as much as possible. After about ten minutes, she emerged and had done the best job she could, but her beautiful outfit was still a mess.

She got herself another coffee, went to the checkout, still fuming from the incident, threw a $20 bill at the young girl serving and waited impatiently to receive her change. The young girl, just trying to be polite, asked: "Oh, did you spill something?" The angry lady was not amused at this question and snapped back with a sarcastic reply: "Oh, you're brilliant! How could you tell I spilt something? You're so brilliant? I guess that's why they pay you the big bucks! Now, give me my change and let me get out of here."

A little shaken from this sarcastic and angry response, the young girl looked in the cash register and, because the store had only just opened, there was no change. She timidly said:, "I've only just opened the store, and we don't have change. I will have to go out back and get some, sorry." With that, the lady launched off into yet another tirade: "I can't believe it! You shouldn't open the shop if you are not ready for business. Just forget about it. I won't be back!" She put down her coffee, snatched the $20 bill back off the young girl, and stormed out of the shop.

The young girl, visibly shaken from this unpleasant encounter, watched as the lady stomped off, got in her car, with her name plastered all over it, and drove off. The penny then dropped for this young girl because that name rang a bell. She ran to the phone, picked it up, dialled and waited for it to answer.

"Hello, Grandpa. You are selling your farm today, aren't you? You are using the realtor [name], aren't you? Okay, can you cancel the deal with her? She came into the shop today, and she was so mean to me, and she said horrible things! You <u>will</u> cancel it, won't you? Good, Grandpa. Thanks. I love you."

The young girl hung up the phone and said, out aloud: "That will teach her to be mean to me".

Because it was a small country town, the man narrating this story knew the girl's grandfather. He knew the price of the property that was about to be sold, and he knew the commission the agent would have received because of the sale. It was a two-million-dollar sale, and the commission was ten per cent. So, in just thirty seconds, because she had an attitude that was very much dependent on her circumstances and zero emotional intelligence, she flushed $200,000 down the toilet.

But wait a minute, I know I said she lost more than one million dollars in thirty seconds at the start of this story. Where did the other $800,000+ come from? Great question. Well, consider how many other people that young girl would have talked to about her experience? What about the grandfather? Who would he have shared the story with about how this realtor treated his precious granddaughter? Can you see where this is leading? The word would ripple out, the reputation of this lady would spread. As a result, the loss of commission on sales over many weeks, months and even years would add up to more than one million dollars. All because she couldn't manage her emotions in one unfortunate thirty-second interaction.

I think it is fair to say, our emotional state will determine the quality and outcomes of our life. That being the case, isn't it worth making the changes you need to make to become a very emotionally intelligent person? Consider the above story and imagine how it may have played out if the realtor had taken the time to develop emotional intelligence, and an attitude independent of circumstances? Well, let's have some fun with it, shall we?

Imagine her driving along when the old man in the pick-up truck pulls out in front of her. She swerves, slams on her brakes, spills coffee all over her beautiful cream outfit and comes to rest on the side of the road. Instead of getting angry and abusive, what if she thought: *'Wow, that was a close call. I am so glad I missed a collision and that we are both okay.'* When she went to the convenience store to clean up and buy her coffee, what if she had a different answer and tone when asked by the young girl: "Oh, did you spill something?" What if instead, she answered: "Yes, I did, but it will clean up. It's not a big deal. I have many more important things to do today to worry about a little stain. I must get out and help people. By the way, thanks for asking."

How would the young girl have felt after this hypothetical interaction, as opposed to the actual one? After watching the lady leave, she may have identified her by the name and picture on her car, then rang her grandfather with a very different message. It may have been something like this:

"Hello, Grandpa. You are selling your farm, aren't you? You are using the realtor [name], aren't you? Okay, can you really look after her and even recommend her to your friends. She came into the shop today and was very nice to me, even though she had spilt coffee all over her beautiful cream outfit! You <u>will</u> look after her, won't you? Good, Grandpa. Thanks. I love you."

Maybe the grandfather would have used her for other properties. Maybe he would have referred her and got her more business. Maybe that one interaction would have set up her future. Only if she had some emotional intelligence and an attitude independent of circumstances. Instead of setting up her prosperous future, her lack of emotional intelligence destroyed it for her. That's the difference one thirty-second interaction can make in your life. It's the difference between taking control of your emotional state and using it to create abundance in your life or not.

Moving towards 'TEARS of Joy'

> Proverbs 12:18 – *There is one whose rash words are like sword thrusts, but the tongue of the wise brings healing.* (ESV)

E-motion, as defined in the last chapter, means to excite or agitate into motion. The direction of that motion and the impact it will have on your life depends on the nature of the agitation or excitement. I think I have covered that in enough detail in this chapter and the previous one. I do need to emphasise one thing, and ask you to consider the following question. What if the major precursor to the action that will take you up to wonderful joy and fulfilment in life, or down to the depths of despair, is emotion? Would it be worth working on strategies to ensure the upwards growth, success, and joy in your life? That's what this chapter has been all about.

I think it is important to believe emotional intelligence will get you much further and faster in life than intellect, knowledge, talent, or ability ever will or can. Earlier in the book, I told the story of a fourteen-year-old boy who thought he was dumb. This thought and belief moved him to feelings of frustration, anger, and helplessness that resulted in the grades reinforcing to him that he was dumb. In fact, it was not intellect. When I asked him if he wanted to change, he said yes. When I asked him if he was willing to work at it consistently, he said yes. When I asked him if he was ready and willing to start today, he said yes. Then I told him: "You are not dumb. In fact, you are one of the smartest people I know. Intelligence is not a reflection of what you know. It's all about what you do."

This is the key to emotional intelligence and using your emotions for good rather than evil. It is about the willingness to believe that you are enough. This is not easy but needs to happen. It is about your willingness to capture emotion, validate it, and then deal with it. It will take some deliberate focus but will change your life. It is about having faith in what you cannot see and knowing everything will work out. This can be uncomfortable and unfamiliar but will give you peace and positivity. Finally, it takes having an attitude independent of circumstances. If you can get the others right, this last one will pretty much take care of itself. Just know and believe this: *Things don't happen to you – they happen for you!*

Key questions and action steps

1. Do you feel your emotional state is in control or out of control more times than not?
2. Are you ready to work on harnessing your emotions for positive outcomes in life? It will take work and focus, so again, I ask, are you prepared to work on harnessing your emotions for positive outcomes in life?
3. Watch some of Marissa Peers videos and then do what she suggests. In other words, put the statement *'I am enough'* everywhere that will be in your vision. Put it on your phone, your fridge, your toilet door, your bathroom mirror, in your car, in your diary. Read it out loud to yourself every time you see it. As soon

as you feel you are good enough, you will be a more positive and optimistic person.

4. Get very deliberate and focused on capturing emotion. Bring it to the light, validate it (you are okay), determine the thought, belief, or perspective that is causing it. If necessary, change your focus. This will take practice and persistence, but it is a game-changer.

5. Find a faith platform you are comfortable with, then hand all your stress and worries over to it and feel the weight of the world lift off your shoulders.

6. Work hard to develop an attitude independent of circumstances. In other words, look for the good in every situation, no matter how bad it may seem. Again, this will take time, focus, and resisting what is normal for you.

7. Finally, when things happen in your life that, on the surface, may seem undesirable, just believe it is happening for you to help you become better, not to you.

CHAPTER 10

Spontaneous action – taking the first step

"I am not talking about considered action, and I am not even talking about logical action. I am talking about spontaneous and instantaneous action."

Nothing moves if nothing moves. Nothing happens if nothing happens. Nothing works if nothing works. These three statements are blindingly obvious. Yet I know far too many people who try to affirm, visualise, think, and feel themselves to succeed in life without taking the most important of all steps, the first. We are getting sold inaccurate information about success from many people profiting from an all-too-common human characteristic. That is, wanting to achieve great things without doing the work. Upfront, I must tell you that nothing will happen in your life if you don't act. Sorry!

Using one specific example, we have been irresponsibly sold the *law of attraction* as the magical answer to all our dreams. In fact, a popular docu-movie, which shall remain nameless, was released in 2006 and perpetuated, I believe, a very misleading and dangerous message. It took the concept of the law of attraction and stated that *you will attract into your life anything that you give attention and focus to.* Now, don't get me wrong, I believe in my God and absolutely buy into the law of attraction. However, the magic is not just praying, thinking, focusing, and paying attention to what you want in your life.

The docu-movie mentioned above talked about the power of affirmation. One example stated that if you simply start affirming that *'unexpected cheques arrive in the mail',* then money will magically appear in your mailbox. This will happen even as you sit on your couch watching TV, doing nothing but chanting this miraculous affirmation. Again, don't get me wrong. I believe in, practice, and teach daily affirmation. In fact, as you know, I wrote about this powerful mindset shifting tool in Chapter 5. However, an affirmation not accompanied by action is like driving an amazing car with no petrol. Make no mistake about it. The magic is in focused and positively expectant action.

As we move into the **A** part of the 'TEARS of joy' model, it is important to know positive thoughts and powerful emotions will help you feel happy and peaceful. However, they won't help you live your optimal life unless followed by directed, purposeful, and immediate action. In this chapter, I am not talking about considered action. I am not referring to planned and perfectly executed action, and I am not even talking about logical action. I am talking about faith-filled, spontaneous, and instantaneous action. Yes, that means now!

I am grateful to have a character trait that leads me into action spontaneously, without over-analysis. Many people, I believe, spend too much time in their own head thinking about, planning, weighing up the pros and cons, talking themselves in and then back out of taking immediate action. Can you relate to this? If you can, what I am about to say will be confronting, unfamiliar and uncomfortable for you. I suggest you stop thinking, stop analysing, stop debating, and start acting, NOW! Even if you don't have all the answers or know what to do.

Many people have the challenge of over-analysis. Our brain is an amazing organ and allows us to create and develop wonderful ideas and solve seemingly impossible problems. However, staying in your head too long is a fatal error. The longer you stay in your head, the longer you will come up with all the reasons why it will be too hard, take too long, you don't have the time, you're not good enough, and blah, blah, blah! My suggestion is that when the idea comes into your head, get it out quickly and move it to your heart. Then, my friend, go with the powerfully positive feeling and take immediate and spontaneous action.

I hear you asking: '*but what if I stuff up, make a mistake, or choose the wrong direction?*' Great question. The answer is, you will at times, so embrace it, learn from it, and then take the next step. Let me tell you, my life is littered with spontaneous actions that led to glorious stuff-ups and wonderful lessons that have shaped who I am, and helped me get to where I wanted to be, right here. Don't be afraid of acting and getting it wrong, be far more afraid of never acting in the first place.

When asked how it felt to fail over 10,000 times in his attempt to invent the electric light bulb, Thomas Edison answered: "I have not failed once. I've just found 10,000 ways that won't work." He then went on to say: "The electric light bulb has caused me the greatest amount of study and has required the most elaborate experiments. Although I was never discouraged or hopeless of its success, I cannot say the same for my associates. Through all the years of experimenting with it, I never once made an associated discovery. It was *deductive*. The results I achieved were the consequence of invention – pure and simple. I would construct and work along various lines until I found them untenable. When one theory was discarded, I developed another at once. I realised very early that this was the only possible way to work out all the problems."

During my trip to the USA in 2019, I spoke to a group in San Francisco about finding meaning and living on purpose. A young lady, Megan, spoke openly about her growing feeling of dissatisfaction with her current job. She wanted to change and start chasing something more fulfilling and meaningful, but she was terrified of taking the risk and getting it wrong. I talked to her about stepping out in faith, as I mentioned in the last chapter. Her main fear was acting without really knowing which way to go, so I told her and the group a story about a father and his young son on a plane trip.

One evening, a father took his young son on a plane for the first time to fly from Melbourne to Sydney. The young boy was a little nervous as the plane taxied to take-off, but seemed to relax after the plane lifted off, moved through the clouds, and cruised at its desired altitude. It was night, there was not much to see out the window, so the young boy started feeling a little bored. At that moment, he got a quizzical look on his face and asked his father: "Dad, how can the pilot see at night?"

"There are headlights on the plane, so the pilot can see," his father replied. This satisfied the boy for a while until he asked: "Dad, how far do the headlights shine?" Now the father was getting a little concerned as to where this conversation was heading but answered: "About 200 metres (300 yards)". The boy considered this answer for a short time and then asked: "And how far is it from Melbourne to Sydney?" The father, starting to squirm in his seat a little, responded: "It's 1,000 kilometres (600 miles) to Sydney".

The father watched the little boy's face as he could see his brain trying to do the calculation. So, the father was expecting the next question. The boy asked: "Dad if it's 1,000 kilometres to Sydney, and the headlights only reach 200 metres, what happens when the plane gets to the end of the 200 metres, and how can the pilot see all the way to Sydney?" The father looked at his concerned little boy and said: "It's okay, son. When the plane gets to the end of 200 metres, the headlights will shine another 200 metres ahead. Every 200 metres we travel, the lights will keep shining another 200 metres further on."

Relating this story back to the fearful Megan, I just encouraged her to take the first step, even though she wasn't 100 per cent clear on where she was going. She could not see the whole journey, but I explained the path would open itself up to her with each step she takes. I think it helped, and I hope, for her sake, she has taken the first step, that spontaneous action that will get the journey started.

One of the most famous and well-used quotes of all time is: *'The journey of one thousand miles begins with a single step'*. It is clichéd, it is over-used, it is also true and critical for success in life. Spontaneity scares some people, but to me, it's who I am, and for that, I am very grateful. I would never have played professional sport without it. I would never have become a teacher, which led me to personal training, without it. I would never have made the crazy decision to buy a café and try and combine it with an eighty-hour per week personal training career, without my action first and think later attitude. And, for me, the greatest and most fulfilling professional achievement in my life, becoming an author, came from an illogical, irrational, and totally spontaneous decision to write my first book.

Let me talk you through the mind of a spontaneous and often illogical action-taker. That is me. I will elaborate on one story that has most profoundly and positively impacted my life and helped me find my own purpose. As I write this today, I have seven published books and, if you are reading this, I have at least eight. If you knew me before I wrote my first book, you would have said, like I did, that the chances of Andrew Jobling being a successful best-selling author are zero.

From as early as I can remember, my dream was to play football at the highest level. As a child, all my thoughts, focus, and energy went into that pursuit. It was my sole driver, to the exclusion of school, studying, reading and, although embarrassed to admit it, girls. I went to a coeducational college, which was an all-girls school only a few short years earlier. So, yes, the girl to boy ratio was very favourable for teenage boys!

I could get a girlfriend. I just couldn't keep the relationship. The protocol was clear. At recess and lunchtime, hanging out with my new girlfriend was expected. Somehow, in most breaks, I found myself playing football, and I neglected my serious boyfriend duties. Consequently, I got used to hearing the words: *'You are dumped!'*

At that time of my life, it didn't bother me. I knew there would be plenty of time for girls when I was a famous footballer. My focus was always football, and I would often get berated by teachers who would ask me where I was heading in life and what I was doing. I would say with confidence and certainty: "I'm going to be a footballer!" I didn't see the need for education. I was going to be a footballer – no brains required! In fact, the only reason I got through school was pride and not wanting to fail. Some extra help from a tutor in my worst subject by far, English, was what got me through with little to spare.

After my schooling was complete, I decided I would give up reading. I mistakenly believed it was no longer necessary in my life, except for the important stuff, the sports section of the newspaper and comics. I stood firm in this belief for many years. That was until about ten years into my personal training career when I decided to learn about nutrition. Why? Because my attempts to get people to train like elite athletes were failing miserably, and I knew something was missing from my limited armoury!

So, I started reading again, and, surprise, surprise, I began learning and getting inspired. Over the next couple of years, I transformed my knowledge and thinking. I was excited about the message I had to share with others. How was I going to do it? That was my main question. Now remember, I am a spontaneous and often illogical action-taker. As crazy as it seemed, my first thought was to buy a café and create a place where people could eat, learn, and live healthier lives. The fact that I was already working eighty hours per week in my personal training business didn't influence my decision. The fact that I had no hospitality experience was not a determining factor. I had a vision, I got excited, and I took immediate action.

Two years later, I deeply regretted that decision and the ensuing action and learned an expensive lesson. In addition to working more than 100 hours per week in both businesses, I ended up close to $100,000 in debt, as the café was losing money day after day after day. I then found myself in the process of trying to sell the café, sitting in the back office staring at my rapidly diminishing bank balance on the computer screen. I was run down, discouraged, delirious, and just hoping that money would magically appear from somewhere. Instead of money arriving in my bank account from somewhere, an idea came into my head. Where this idea came from, I don't know.

That idea was to write a book. As I have already stated several times, it was not a logical or even rational thought. I could, however, see the possibility of it being the answer I was looking for in my life. The answer to how I would get my message out to the world, the answer to loving my life, and the answer to my financial woes. So although I had no idea what writing a book looked like, how to start, or any idea how to get it done, I had, at that moment, decided I would be a bestselling author. The thought went very quickly from my head to my heart. I immediately, without any further analysis, took the first uncertain step.

Make no mistake about it. Immediate action is why I wrote that book and why I am where I am today. It was that crazy, illogical, unreasonable, and spontaneous first step that launched me in a direction I could not be more excited about and grateful for. Once I started, I became more excited and more confident. With each word I wrote, and each action I took, the idea of writing this book went from impossible to possible, from possible to probable, and probable to certain. This totally illogical thought transformed into clear logic with each day that passed and each small action step I took.

As I look back to all the illogical and spontaneous choices I have made in my life, I can see how they all moved me to where I am today. I now see the $100,000 I lost in my café as not a loss at all. Instead I see it as a small and necessary investment that led me to the moment of the irrational decision to write a book. Over the last two decades, I have experienced joy, found purpose, and earned money which makes me feel nothing but gratitude for everything I put into that café. It was the prerequisite of investment, learning, resilience, and growth to become the person I am, and love the life I am living today.

It's about now and, as passionately as I can, I want to tell you that logic is often the killer of creativity and success. Too many people *logically* analyse their idea or aspiration before any action is taken. The tragedy is that most will talk themselves out of taking that first step because of what they justify as *logical reasoning*. Logic has nothing to do with success. Belief, action, and persistence is the key. Unless you have irrefutable evidence that you cannot achieve the desire and aspiration you have in your heart, then it is possible. In fact, with belief and action, it is not just likely, it is predictable. In my case, it wasn't that I knew I could be an author, I just didn't know that I couldn't, and that was enough for me to get started. The rest came down to spontaneous action and faith.

As I have already discussed several times, Phillip Yancey's definition of faith is so apt in my life: '*faith means trusting in advance what will only make sense in reverse*'. It is such an important part of life and achievement that I must mention it again. When you finally achieve what you want, even if you had no idea how it would happen when you started, it will make total sense and seem logical.

Before I found God, I already believed in the Universe and in the concept of faith. This has been a significant reason for many actions I have taken that have shaped my life. I now know that God has been the orchestrator of my life. I may not have known the way forward when I took the spontaneous action and started many of my aspirations.

However, God knew and led me to the place I wanted to and needed to be. Believing that without question or logic is true God-given faith. I want to encourage you to also believe.

When you hear people say anything is possible, sometimes it can be hard to believe, right? It's hard to believe because we are not operating in faith but logic. While I absolutely believe that anything is possible for you, the condition to turn this possibility into reality is to take that first step in faith. Stop thinking, analysing, doubting, stressing, and worrying, and act <u>today</u>.

Moving towards 'TEARS of Joy'

> Joshua 1:9 – *Have I not commanded you? Be strong and courageous. Do not be frightened, and do not be dismayed, for the LORD your God is with you wherever you go.* (ESV)

To sit at the bottom of the mountain, looking at the very top, wondering how to get there, will terrify the most courageous of people. Of course you need to have a vision and set a goal to reach the summit. When your vision and goal are locked in the vault, and you are committed, take your eyes off the summit, and focus on the first immediate step. The only way to get to the top of a mountain is one step at a time. The only way to write a book is one word at a time. The only way to build a strong relationship is one loving act at a time. The only way to build wealth is by earning and saving one day at a time. The only way to create a successful business is one phone call at a time.

Are you getting me? Right now, forget about all the steps that it will take, and just focus on one, the first. The first step is never easy because you are overcoming *inertia*, which means *a tendency to do nothing or to remain unchanged.* You increase your chances of making this first crazy, spontaneous, even illogical step a reality by following the first two parts of the 'TEARS of joy' model.

Think about what you want, why you want it, why you <u>can</u> do it, that it is possible and how it will feel when you have achieved it. As that thought transmutes itself into a fleeting but powerful, positive feeling or emotion, act immediately. Don't wait, don't put it off until tomorrow, and don't expect that motivation to last. ACT NOW with faith! That first step will get you moving, give you confidence, empower you, unlock the secrets to the next step, and start the journey to the next part of the 'TEARS of joy' model, **R**outine.

Key questions and action steps

1. Would you consider yourself an action-taker or an over-thinker?
2. What are the benefits and disadvantages of your main character trait?
3. If you are an over-analyser, would you be open to starting to be more spontaneous?
4. What would be the worst-case scenario if you did? What about if you didn't?
5. What would be the best-case scenario?
6. Can you see why acting today is critical in the pursuit of creating 'TEARS of joy' in your life?
7. What action are you willing to take TODAY before you go to bed?
8. When you have done it, celebrate because you have *won the day*, and then do it again tomorrow. I will talk more about winning the day later in the book.
9. Is it a deal?
10. Take action, NOW!

CHAPTER 11

Developing spontaneity

*"Don't aim to get to the top or to the end.
Just make the first step the goal."*

In the last chapter, I hope I impressed upon you the critical importance of taking the first step today. Just know that the choice not to act is a thought that will create a negative emotion that will lead to the action or inaction, as the case may be, which will lead you… nowhere! Therefore, if you are an analytical over-thinker, this chapter is vital for you to read, absorb and act on. Yes, I encourage you to act on it. Yes, I mean today. Yes, I mean without having all the answers. I understand this will be a challenge for you, but I want to encourage you to work with me.

In this book, and through my 'TEARS of joy' model, you will have picked up that I'm suggesting emotion leads to action. Some people may disagree, maybe even you. There is a bit of a debate about whether emotion determines action <u>or</u> action determines emotion. So, which is correct? That is a great question.

The great answer is BOTH. Confused?

Even when you don't feel like it, there is no doubt taking positive action will lead to strong and positive emotions. This will reinforce the action and increase the chances of repeated action. The key question I am focusing on is, what gets us taking that initial action in the first place? It is my belief, even if we don't want to, are scared to, or couldn't be bothered to act, the thing that will initiate spontaneous action is a positive feeling. It may be just an instantaneous, momentary, or fleeting feeling. It doesn't matter, as long as it initiates the spontaneous action I discussed in the previous chapter. Once the first action is taken, it will lead to more positive feelings that will help you to take the next step, and the next, and the next.

It may be faith. It may be love. It may be determination. It may be a strong desire. It may simply be hope. The reality is action leads to reinforcing the right feelings we need to keep going. It is, however, an emotion that will always be responsible for the initial and most important action to happen. I hope that clears up what may seem to be a paradox. Just know the right emotions and the right actions will continually feed each other to help you create any outcome you want – on the condition you first get started.

If you are like me and take spontaneous action, then you will enjoy this chapter. I hope you get additional benefits to enable you to take the actions that will most often lead to the result you want, rather than an expensive lesson. If you are anything like I was, you will give anything a go, often without any idea of the consequences. This is not the spontaneous action I am talking about. So you may, like I did, have to add just a little – and I said a little – bit of reflection into your action-taking. I have learned this the hard way through some expensive lessons.

Because of very little thought for the consequences, I invested a large sum of money into owning a part-share of a racehorse. That was an expensive way to learn that anything eating while you sleep is bad for your bank account! A lesson I really didn't need to learn. I also did minimal due diligence before investing in the share market, not once but twice. Both times, I ended up losing a lot of money. I did not reflect after my first loss, and so didn't learn anything from the experience. After my second failure, I learned not to invest in the share market, which is probably not the lesson I should have learned. However, after those two experiences, it's the one that I walked away with.

I have spoken about the café. While some reflection and prior knowledge of hospitality would have been useful before I risked and lost close to $100,000, I am grateful for that experience. Why? You may well ask. Because, if not for the failure and the resulting questioning of how I would make my mark and get my message out to the world, I don't think I would ever have made the decision to write my first book. As I write this book, that one decision has had the greatest positive flow-on effect in my life for almost twenty years.

So, action is the only thing that will move you towards what you want. In addition, some reflection before you act today is advised. This will help you to avoid some horribly wrong choices, like some that I have made. This chapter is devoted to helping you with some strategies for becoming a more spontaneous action-taker. Those dreams in your head will become an incredible reality in your life. It is possible, and you can do it, but you need to start today.

Vision and desire

If we know action is the result of emotion, and positive and immediate action will happen when there is a strong positive emotional force, then we need to focus every day on what will help us feel positive, empowered, and determined. The clearer your vision for your purpose and the type of life you want to live, the more driven you will become to act. I still remember the feeling, almost twenty years ago, when I had the vision to become an author and live a different life from the one I was living. The feeling of excitement and determination drove me into action. In my mind, I thought that if I want to live this amazing life, and becoming an author will be the way it will happen, then why would I want to waste any time? I got started immediately.

It is common to have a fleeting vision, followed by a burst of excited energy and then, when distractions take over, allow it to get buried in the busyness of life. This happens all too often for far too many people. The key to enabling the desire for a strong vision to stay with you and keep you moving forward is to put it in your face every day. Get your vision board on the wall where you can see it. Put up pictures and affirmations around your house, in your car, on your computer and on your phone. Feed that dream every day by imagining, reading, visiting, test-driving, and living it in your mind and heart. Without a deliberate focus on what you want and the associated emotions that go with that, taking the action you need to take each and every day will just not happen.

Believe you are an action-taker

You cannot outwork lack of belief. If you start acting, but deep down, you believe you are a procrastinator, guess what will win out in the end? Why? Because what do procrastinators do? They put things off! You need to start affirming, speaking into your life, and believing you are an action-taker. This is because no matter what you attempt to do, that voice in your head will win out in the end. Make sure it is saying what you want. Your inner beliefs and philosophy will always dictate your long-term results. It is essential that the action you are taking is backed up by a strong belief that you are the type of person who will act, persist, and win.

When I decided to write my first book, do you honestly think I believed I was a writer? Not a chance, but I did know if I started with the belief that I'm not a writer, I would have sabotaged myself early in the process. Sometimes you must manipulate your own thinking, which is what I did. I didn't necessarily believe I was a writer, but I knew I was a great communicator. Therefore, I knew I could get my message across. I believed if I could speak the words, I could write them, and that belief, coupled with daily action, got me here. Even today, when people introduce me as a writer, I tell them I'm not a writer. I am an author. When you start to change your inner beliefs about who you are and what you do, you will start doing and keep doing those things.

Faith

Yes, I am coming back here again. Why? Because, after more than half a century on this planet, years of doubt, too much anxiety and worry and, getting stuck far too often, I have realised this is a missing piece of the success puzzle for most people. What stops most people from taking the first step? Doubt, fear, anxiety, and worry, right? They doubt they can do it when they have never even tried. They fear the worst outcome when the chances of it happening are negligible to none. They are anxious about making a mistake when mistakes are good things that will lead to learning, improvement, and success. They worry about looking stupid when it looks more stupid doing nothing. We have all been there, haven't we?

Faith, and I mean true faith, removes the barriers to acting and creating astronomical success. Again, I will bore you with my favourite quotes – *'faith means trusting in advance what will only make sense in reverse'* and *'faith is the substance of things hoped for, the evidence of things not yet seen'*.

I talked to a large group of nurses in St Louis, USA, in 2019 and spoke about faith as one of the seven pieces of the puzzle I talk about in my book, *The Wellness Puzzle*. I asked them to raise their hand if they had achieved something in their lives that they were proud of. They all raised their hands. I then asked them to leave their hands up if they didn't know how they would achieve the goal when they started. Guess what? They all, and I mean all, left their hands in the air. I imagine the same could be said for something you have achieved. Right? What is it that moved you to the achievement? That, my friend, is faith!

If you are a Christian, you believe that God will guide you. If you are Buddhist or Hindu, you believe your path is set. If you believe in the Universe, you believe the law that states, what you give out, you will get back. If you just believe in karma and do the right things, you will get the results you want. No matter your platform of faith, trust me, it will destroy doubt, fear, anxiety, and worry and clear the path for you to take that first and most important spontaneous step. The leap of faith.

Find just twenty seconds of insane courage

Benjamin Mee was portrayed in the movie, **We Bought a Zoo.** At one point in the movie, he encouraged his teenage son to talk to the girl he liked. His advice was: "You know, sometimes all you need is twenty seconds of insane courage, just literally twenty seconds of embarrassing bravery, and I promise you something great will come of it". Now I don't know if Benjamin said this to his son in real life, or if it was just Hollywood hype, but it is a wonderful mantra to live by. We all can find and display just twenty seconds of insane courage and, as Benjamin says, something great will always come of it.

Think about what could come about from the twenty seconds of courage that it takes to get out of bed and go for a walk when it's cold outside, make the phone call to ask for help and expose your vulnerability, audition for the show even with the risk of not being selected, make a terrifying sales call you've been putting off, ask that person out on a date and risk rejection, or any of the other things you could do in that short but life-changing twenty-second period of time.

About six months after my decision to write a book, I had somehow found time in my crazy life and completed the 50,000-word manuscript for *Eat Chocolate, Drink Alcohol and be Lean & Healthy*. After several edits and re-writes, it was now the best I could make it, based on my limited literary skills. The next step was to start submitting it to publishers. I went through the first publisher's website and followed all the submission guidelines to a tee. I wrote a synopsis, a query letter, printed out the first few chapters of the book, put it all in an envelope, put a stamp on it, and it was ready to send.

Yes, I said to send in the everyday postal service. This was how most manuscripts were submitted back then. I had that package sitting on my desk, ready to put it in a mailbox, for days. Every time I walked into my office, there it was, just waiting to be posted. Every time I would look at it, I felt fear in the pit of my gut and would say to myself: '*I'll post it later*'. I was terrified. Why? Because I had a fear, my worst nightmare would come true. The fear that the book wasn't good enough, and I didn't want to see those words written in a rejection letter.

After about a week, I put it in my car to post the next time I was out running errands. It sat in my car for about another week, even though there were many opportunities to post it during that time. The fear of rejection was holding me back. Finally, after many days, I thought: '*just twenty seconds of insane courage, just literally twenty seconds of embarrassing bravery, and something great will come of it*'. So, I went to the closest post box, and it took less than twenty seconds to get out of my car, place that package in the mailbox, and it was on its way. Well, as you already know, that twenty seconds of insane courage did lead to something great. In fact, it transformed my life.

Act like a robot

As much as I would like to think it's easy to change the emotional state that predictably leads us into spontaneous action and gets us moving towards our purpose in life, I am not that naïve – anymore, that is! It is simple, but it's far from easy, and sometimes, even for me, my thoughts are not moving me to feel excited and empowered about certain things I need to do. That being the case, how then do we take that immediate action when our thoughts and emotions are resisting and holding us back? Good question, and I have a great answer. Just switch off your emotional control and switch into an automated robot mode.

Okay, so what does that mean? Think about how robots operate, or maybe computers if getting your head around a robot is challenging. They are programmed to predictably complete tasks, and there is no emotion involved, right? You turn them on, give them an instruction, and they are programmed to complete the task. With this in mind, let me tell you how I can get up and exercise every morning when I would often much rather stay in bed. My alarm is set for 5:15 am, and my goal is to get up and exercise. I am always motivated and excited about exercising when I go to sleep. However, sometime during the eight hours I am sleeping, that excitement evaporates. So, when I wake up, the last thing I often feel like doing is exercise.

At that point, I deliberately switch off my emotional control. In other words, I stop thinking, I click into robot mode and, before I have time to talk myself out of it, I've thrown back the covers, placed my feet on the floor and am out of bed. Irrespective of how I feel, I simply keep myself moving, to the bathroom, to the kitchen, into my training gear. Before I know it, I am out the door and running. Once running, I start to get into the feeling, it becomes easier to keep going, and I get my training session done. Then, when the session is done, I always feel incredible, and I am so glad I got up and did it. Thanks to the robot mode I'm able to tap into.

I use this strategy for other things, like writing, phone calls that are challenging, paying bills, cleaning, and any other task where I can't change my thinking and emotional state. What about you? You don't have to love or be excited about everything to help you achieve what you desire. You just must do them. Isn't that great news? When you finally get to the point and realise success comes from acting on things that can be uncomfortable and not always fun, things will change for you. When you can switch out of, *I just don't feel like it* mode, and into *I will do it robotically anyway* mode, success and happiness are yours for the taking.

Focus on the best-case scenario

I have the privilege of meeting, associating, helping, and working with some wonderful people. One of the most inspiring young ladies I know is Heather Rendulic. From a young age, she suffered from a severe brain condition called *Cavernous Angioma*, which consists of weak blood vessels in the brain. This lesion would often bleed and, over eleven months led to paralysis and ultimately a nine-hour emergency craniotomy to remove the lesion from her brain. The prognosis for her recovery was not optimistic, and whether she would walk, or function normally again was doubtful.

After marathon surgery, her mother, father, and sister were waiting in the recovery room for her to come out of the anaesthetic. Heather had half her head shaved, a long scar on her skull and had tubes of all sorts coming out of her body to keep her alive, so they were understandably concerned. Her older sister, who was to be married six months later, was specially upset and sobbing for Heather. Now, it's important to note Heather is a devout Christian with unshakeable faith.

As Heather woke up from the anaesthetic, the first person she saw and heard was her sister. She saw how upset her sister was, she held out her hand to her, and then the first words that came out of her mouth after her nine-hour surgery, were: "Oh, stop your crying. I'll be dancing at your wedding!" Six months later, despite her condition and despite the doctor's assessment of her recovery, Heather was dancing at her sister's wedding!

What was the magic that helped Heather achieve that miracle and create the amazing memory in her and her sister's life? Doctors told her it would not be possible, so how did she make it happen? When Heather came out of the anaesthetic and saw her sister sobbing, she thought about and visualised the best-case scenario. She imagined herself dancing at her sister's wedding and could see the smile on her sister's face. That vision and the powerful emotion it released got her into action to start the rehabilitation process.

Every day, and with every challenge Heather faced, she stayed focused on that picture in her head. It kept her going, and it kept her getting up after each fall. We can all choose to focus on the best-case scenario. We can all get a powerful and compelling picture in our heads of what we want. With that clarity and the emotion that comes with it, taking that first spontaneous action will happen naturally.

Heather is one of the most inspiring people I know. I spent some incredible time with her and her amazing parents, Lynn and Randy, in Pittsburgh in 2019. We spoke together at several events. Now she is the author of *Headstrong*, a book that describes her courageous journey and is an uplifting read for anyone looking to overcome challenges in their life.

Think about the worst-case scenario

I will always recommend that you focus on what you want and the best possible scenario, as Heather did. I understand there are sceptics and doubters in the world and, to be honest, that was me for much of my life. It may also be you. That being the case, try this strategy – think about the worst possible scenario. If it's something you can live with then just get moving. If the worst-case scenario is getting decapitated, ending up in jail, losing all your money, or hurting another person, then maybe you should re-think your plan. But, if it's bearable, then why not give it a go anyway?

For me, I was excited about the thought of becoming an author. However, I clearly had doubts about whether I could do it. When I stopped and thought about the worst-case scenario, which was being rejected and not being an author, it was not the end of the world. That was enough for me to think, *why not just give it a go?* After I published my first book, I was still working eighty-plus hours per week as a personal trainer and wanted to retire from it. I came across an e-commerce business that could help me do just that. The best-case scenario was amazing. The worst-case scenario was bearable. So, I gave it a go, and incredibly, two years later, I retired from personal training after fifteen years of working eighty-hours-per-week.

When you have a mission, a purpose and/or a dream, there is nothing bad about giving it a go, even if it ends up being the wrong choice. Any action is better than no action. As devastating as it was to spend two years in a café that stole my time, my relationships, and my money, I would not be sitting here writing my eighth book if I didn't just go with that crazy idea. The worst-case scenario, in this case, happened. In fact, it was even worse than what I would have imagined when I started. Even though it did, I survived, I learned, I changed strategy, and as a result, I ended up on exactly the path I didn't even know, at that time, I wanted to be on. Go on, get started now.

Just focus on, and worry about, the first step

I truly believe what stops most people is the lack of belief they can go the distance. Whether this is writing the book, building the business, recovering ailing health, making the team, getting the job, running that marathon, impacting millions of lives, or whatever the vision may be. We all too often stand at the bottom of the mountain, look up at the top and think about how high it is, how hard it will be and how long it will take, and we convince ourselves it's not for us. However, if we truly knew and believed that climbing a mountain happens just one step at a time, and we just set a goal to take the first step, more steps would be taken all around the world in the direction of people's dreams.

As I write this chapter, I recently had a conversation with transformational coach Sean O'Leary on *The Wellness Puzzle Podcast*. It was titled, *Just, the next step*. Sean calls himself the *Transformed Man* and started his journey at 135 kg (300 lbs). He had kidney issues, was verging on diabetes, and had pain in pretty much every part of his body. Within twelve weeks, Sean had dropped five clothes sizes and transformed into a purpose-driven man who is now lean, energised, and healthy. When he decided to transform his life at his lowest point, he had no idea how it would happen, so he started researching and asking for help.

He was very clear as he explained that his success did not come from motivation, ability, or knowledge of the process but from just taking the next step. He explained about the days he lay in bed for thirty minutes trying to talk himself into getting up to exercise. He spoke about the times he sat in his car outside the gym, trying to convince himself to go in. In the final analysis, he said to himself, *just take the next step*. Just the next step to get out of bed and see what happens. Just the next step to get out of the car, go into the gym and see what happens. With that focus on just the next step, he transformed his life one day at a time.

Don't aim to get to the top or to the end. Just make the first step the goal. You can do that, I can do that, we all can do that. To me, the idea of writing a whole book was terrifying and intimidating, but I knew I could write one word. It's amazing when you set the goal for one simple step, how much easier the next step is. My goal in this chapter is to get you taking that critical first step. Even if it's the only step you ever take, you will be better off than you will be if you don't take that step. It may seem insignificant, but trust me, it's the most significant thing you can do.

Moving towards 'TEARS of Joy'

> Ecclesiastes 11:6 – *Sow your seed in the morning, and at evening let your hands not be idle, for you do not know which will succeed, whether this or that, or whether both will do equally well.* (NIV)

The title of this section of each chapter is, as you can see, ***Moving*** towards *'TEARS of joy'*. The keyword is *moving*. You will never get to the point in your life when you live in a way that fulfils your purpose and provides incredible joy without it. You can't hope yourself, think yourself, affirm yourself, pray yourself, or even motivate yourself to that place. You must act. Too many people believe that motivation, inspiration, and the right timing are the vital ingredients necessary to start moving. It's the other way around. In other words, when you start moving, you will be motivated, inspired, and clear that now is the right time.

As you read back over this chapter, identify one or more of the strategies I have outlined, and commit yourself to the first and most important step. Every day you delay, it will become a habit or routine and lead you to the most unfulfilling, frustrating, and possibly tragic life you can imagine. This is not what anyone wants, yet it's what most people get, simply because the action they choose is inaction.

Win the day is a mantra I would encourage you to adopt and use every day. It's one I will explore in the coming chapters. It will help you to act today and feel good about yourself as a winner. It will increase the odds that you will win the day again the next day and on each day that unfolds in your long, happy, healthy, prosperous, and purpose-driven life. Spontaneity, by definition, means immediate action. As uncomfortable as it might be, that means now, not tomorrow, next week or next year. So, have faith, trust that all will work out the way you want and become a spontaneous action-taker today.

Key questions and action steps

1. Can you see why acting today is the only thing that can move you towards creating 'TEARS of joy' in your life?

2. If you answered yes, are you ready to commit to taking action before you lay your head on the pillow tonight?

3. Let's do a quick and spontaneous exercise right now. Pick up your phone NOW, and send a loving, encouraging, or complimentary message to someone who would value it.

4. Did you do it? How does that feel? Pretty cool, right? See how simple acting is?

5. Look through each of the strategies I have touched on in the chapter and have summarised below. Identify the one or two that most resonate with you.

6. *Vision and desire* – if you haven't already done this, then now is the time. Get clear on what you want in your life, create a vision board, and get a strong emotional attachment to make it a reality. Clarity and strong desire will immediately move you into action.

7. *Believe you're an action taker* – start today to affirm that you are a spontaneous action-taker. Then, take some positive action to reinforce the statement and turn it into a strong belief about yourself.

8. *Faith* – what can I say? Just take a leap of faith and trust that you will land exactly where you need to land to move you in the direction of your best life.

9. *Find twenty seconds of insane courage* – add this to the leap of faith section, and you will be unstoppable.

10. *Act like a robot* – when you know you need to do something, just imagine you're a robot and automatically act before you think too much about it.

11. *Focus on the best-case scenario* – imagine all the dreams you want to come true from this one spontaneous action.

12. *Consider the worst-case scenario* – is it really that bad? Can you deal with it? What opportunities may come with it? Would you rather deal with failure or regret?

13. *Focus on the first step* – don't worry about anything else. Just take the first step and watch the path forward unfold.

14. You know what you need to do, don't you? So, move the idea out of your head and into your heart, and take that first spontaneous, even illogical step, today.

CHAPTER 12

The power of routine

"Unconscious habits will either take you up to amazing success, abundance, love and wellbeing or take you down to the pits of depression, lack, sickness and regret."

Make no mistake about it, what you currently have and what you will end up with in your life, good or bad, results from the habits or routines you develop to the point of unconscious competency. I would rather use the word *habit* instead of *routine*, but 'H' didn't work in the acronym. I mean, 'TEAHS of joy' just doesn't have the same impact, does it? So, from here on, I will oscillate between the words *habit* and *routine* and assume the same meaning for both. Anyway, back on track. Google defines routine as *'performed as part of a regular procedure rather than for a special reason'*. In other words, it's just what we do, and it doesn't require deliberate thought, negotiation, or stress.

However, getting an action to be *performed as part of a regular procedure* will take deliberate thought, negotiation, focus and maybe a little stress for a period. However, the result is so incredibly worth it. More than you may know right now. When you can move positive and life-enhancing actions to the point of unconscious competence, then life is sweet. So, what do I mean by unconscious competence? Do you ever have to think about breathing? Why not? Unconscious competence. Have you ever found yourself standing in front of the bathroom mirror brushing your teeth and then, suddenly, wondered how you even got there? Unconscious competence. Have you ever driven home from work or some other place you drive home from regularly, arrived in your driveway and then thought: *how did I get here? I can't remember the trip at all.* Unconscious competence.

The great news is once unconscious competence is developed, you won't die from lack of oxygen when you are asleep, have your teeth fall out, or get lost on the way home from work. With an unconscious competency and DNA wired routine, any behaviour becomes a fixed pathway in your brain to ensure that it continues to deliver, forever, without conscious thought. Further, any positive behaviour can be developed into an unconscious routine that will continue to bring amazing results into your life. Are you getting excited?

On the flip side, and we need to talk about the flip side, the opposite is true. Do you find yourself biting your nails or reacting badly to certain situations? Do you make poor food choices, procrastinate, or have any other behaviour you know is not necessarily healthy without realising how it happened? Do you find your finger in your mouth, biting that nail, without any conscious recollection of how it got there? Do you find yourself chomping on biscuits, cake, or chocolate, again, before you even know what you're doing? Is it normal for you to react badly to conflict or challenges? Is putting things off your go-to position without any understanding of why? This is also unconscious competence.

You see, unconscious routines will either take you up to amazing success, abundance, love, and wellbeing or take you down to the pits of depression, lack, sickness, and regret. But then, you already know this, right? Please don't despair if you know you have habits that are not serving you. It can all be changed in a heartbeat. Remember, everything starts with a thought, belief, or perspective that you choose to focus on. The goal is to get the behaviours that will take you up to amazing success, abundance, love, and wellbeing to become unconscious daily actions, just like brushing your teeth. Therefore, your goal is to create unconscious competence with the right behaviours. You need to move behaviours from unconscious incompetence to conscious incompetence, then to conscious competence and finally to unconscious competence. I will discuss this in more detail in the next chapter. Right now, I want to make sure you understand the power of unconscious routines in your life.

The reality of true success is that it's not anywhere near as much about talent, intellect, age, luck, or circumstances, as it is about the unconscious routines you choose to create. I say this a lot, but I'm just not sure people listen to or agree with me. Why do I say that? Because, even though I repeat it *ad-nauseam*, I still get the same excuse as to why people don't achieve what they want. That excuse is always: *I'm not good enough, smart enough, strong enough, talented enough or lucky enough.* This is a lie and, if you are saying it to yourself, stop it!

The truth is that success is not about ability, it's about sustainability. Success is not a talent, it's a decision. Anyone can choose to create the daily actions, turn them into unconscious routines that will lead to incredible abundance in any area of life. The mistake most people make is looking at successful actors, athletes, businesspeople, or the like and assume they got there through talent, circumstances, or a lucky break. These people don't see the hours, days, months, and years of struggle, persistence, and action when it didn't seem to be working. It takes years to become an overnight success!

When I was a personal trainer, it amused and aggravated me at the same time when people would tell me how lucky I was. They assumed I was lucky to have the body and fitness I had because of what they considered *good genetics.* What they didn't know was that every single day, I ate well, trained effectively, and committed time to my health and wellbeing, whether I felt like it, wanted to, or not. It had absolutely nothing to do with luck or genetics. It had everything to do with the unconscious routine patterns I chose and worked to develop.

In fact, my genes are a curse to me. I have the opposite problem of many people. My natural *genetic* body type is ectomorphic. Yes, I know you are asking. *What does that mean?* Google describes an Ectomorph in this way:

> An **ectomorph** is a typical skinny guy. Ecto's have a light build with small joints and lean muscle. Usually, **ectomorph's** have long, thin limbs with stringy muscles. Shoulders tend to be thin with little width.

Let me tell you, for a teenager with aspirations to be a successful professional Australian Rules footballer, and wanting to impress the opposite sex, this is not good. The terms *skinny guy, thin limbs, light build, stringy muscles,* and *thin shoulders* were not the ones I wanted to associate with my body! I was so skinny, I had to run around in the shower to get wet! I used to get paid money by bar owners to come and stand around. I was so skinny that I made the drinks look bigger! My nicknames ranged from *the human pipe cleaner* to *a toothpick with ears.* Tragic, but true!

I had to work hard and consistently to prepare myself to play football at the highest level. Let me tell you, putting muscle onto an ectomorphic frame is no easy feat. It took many hours each week of attitude development, strict nutrition, and muscle tearing training to get to reasonable body weight and size. When people tell me they can't change their bodies because of genetics, hormones, age, or many other reasons, I am empathetic, just not sympathetic. It's got far less to do with genes and much more to do with work, focus, determination and, creating suitable routines.

I will talk more about strategies to go about creating great routines in the next chapter. In this chapter, I want you to be sold on the fact and know beyond any shadow of a doubt that nothing of significance is possible without creating the right routines in your life. Yes, it's boring for a period, it's uncomfortable, and it's inconvenient. However, once unconscious competence kicks in, you will never have to negotiate those important actions again. In the short term, you need to focus on creating the routines that will allow amazing, even seemingly impossible, things to happen in your life.

The secret to the routine creation process is clarity and desire about what you want. As a teenager with an aspiration to become a famous footballer, I can see how little I worried about the discomfort, inconvenience, and tedious nature of what I had to do. It excited me because I knew that each action and step would lead me to what I wanted so badly. Many people struggle with taking the actions required to create the habits they need because they focus on the wrong things. They focus on the discomfort, inconvenience, or tediousness of the action rather than the amazing outcome the routines will lead to.

Honestly, if my focus was on how hard training would be, how much it would hurt, and how long it would take me to get into the team, I would have given up before I had even started. Crazy as this may sound, I looked forward to the pain and suffering of training, or at least, how I would feel when the pain and suffering was over. This was because my dream was to be a professional sportsman, and I knew I needed to be supremely fit to make that happen. In the early gut-busting and muscle-melting days, training was never a drag or a burden. It was always a step closer to my vision of running through a banner, onto the ground, in front of 100,000 screaming fans. The habit creation process was never something I questioned, doubted, negotiated, or even consciously considered.

As I am writing this chapter, let me tell you, I didn't really feel like it before I started. However, writing is now an unconscious routine for me. This morning, before I even knew what I was doing, I was (and am) writing. It's just what I do now. The crazy thing is that I only ever write for about fifteen minutes each day. That's about two or three paragraphs per day! You may be asking; *how can he possibly call himself an author when he only writes two or three paragraphs per day?* That is a very reasonable question, and I have an even more impressive answer.

We seem to think that massive action, unreasonable sacrifice, and over-the-top commitment is what's required to create abundant success. Wrong! Have you ever heard about the compounding power of small and consistent actions? As you already know, when I decided to write my first book, I was working more than 100 hours per week. I didn't have large periods of time to immerse myself in writing. I could only create small pockets of time every day. Incredibly, after just four months of making the illogical decision to write a book, I had written 50,000 words. Within two years, I was a published author of two books selling over 100,000 copies! Yes, that sounds almost impossible, but it's all about the compounding effect of a very simple, seemingly insignificant, positive daily action.

In 2017, I made a decision. I decided for myself and my goals, but also to be an example to the people I was mentoring. I decided that, for the entire year of 2017, I would write every single day. Yes, that's 365 days. Now, before then, I was consistent but not writing every single day. My vision was to experience achieving the goal and help my clients create similar habits to get more out of their writing. However, the process provided so much more. I made the decision that I would write at least 500 words each day. For me, that would take between fifteen to thirty minutes, depending on the flow I was in. At the end of the year, on 31 December 2017, I had achieved the goal. In just a meagre fifteen to twenty minutes per day, over that year, I wrote almost 200,000 words, which is equivalent to three or four books!

Would you believe it possible that you could write three to four books in a year? I'm not sure if I would ever have thought it could be done, or that I could do it. It sounds like it would require massive dedication, hours each day, and unreasonable sacrifice that most people would never be willing to make. Nope! It takes only fifteen to thirty minutes per day, every day, and the job is done. Mind-blowing stuff, right? Well, it is for me anyway. That's the incredible power of creating positive and healthy unconscious routines.

Ever since that decision on 1 January 2017, I have written every day and not missed one. Not one. If I maintain this habit for the next fifty years, which I will because I am now an unconsciously competent author, I will write 150 to 200 books in that time. Can you see the incredibly powerful compounding effect of small, seemingly insignificant daily habits?

However, there are times when taking those daily actions and creating unconscious routines may not seem to be doing any good, or getting you closer to what you want. Be very careful not to judge your results too early, or make the mistake of thinking you aren't benefiting because the results aren't there. As I spoke about in Chapter 6, I am grateful for twenty months in my professional football career when nothing seemed to be happening. However, beneath the obvious surface, it was just what I needed to make it at the highest level. I'm glad I hung around to find out just what was destined to happen.

So, let me explain what really happened in those twenty months between August 1983 and April 1985. I was working my brains out to achieve my dream of playing senior professional football. At the time, it seemed like it was taking an eternity. Every session was back-breaking. Every week seemed like a month. Every Thursday night before a game, waiting for teams to be read out, was torture. I had got through the entire 1983 season without being selected for the senior team. I had been working towards being selected, and it was now the last game of the year. The last Thursday night of the year came around, and I sat there, naively waiting in anticipation for the team selection and for my name to be called out. It didn't happen.

As I explained in Chapter 6, an unexpected and last-minute phone call from the coach on the Saturday morning before the last game let me know that I was in the team. So, my first game came by total surprise, in the last round of the 1983 season. It was an amazing experience, I was proud, and I was confident that my successful professional football career was on the verge of exploding. However, I was wrong!

I trained hard during the pre-season period leading into the 1984 season. I was fit, focused and ready to launch and establish my senior professional football career. It was a tough pre-season, but I knew I was ready, so when the Thursday night before the first game came around, I was confident as I sat there waiting for the teams to be announced. I sat right at the front of the room. I was like an excited child on Christmas morning, with my eyes fixed on the senior coach as he read through the list of names that would be representing the club in that first game. He never looked at me, and he never read my name out. My head dropped, my shoulders slumped, and for the briefest of moments, I was devastated.

Not for too long, though, because I knew what I had to do. I had to show up, play well in the reserve grade team that weekend, train hard next week, and make sure I was in the team the following week. So, I did all those things. The following Thursday night, after training rolled around, again I sat right at the front of the room. My eyes were fixed on the senior coach as he read through the list of names that would be representing the club in that second game. Again, he never looked at me, and he never read out my name.

I thought: *'What's going on? I played well, I'm fit, I'm ready. What's their problem?'* But I made the decision again to just show up, play well in the reserve grade team that weekend, train hard that next week, and make sure I was in the team the following week. So, I did, again. And again, I missed the selection. I didn't have to overcome this disappointment for just a just few weeks. The same thing happened for every single week of the 22 games in that whole 1984 season. Every week I showed up, I played well, I trained hard, and I missed selection.

The question I often get asked is: *why did you keep turning up?* The answer is simple because it was what I did. It was a competent unconscious routine that I developed for myself. Initially, I knew that if I continued to show up, one of two things would happen. I would either get selected in the team or be told to leave the club. Either way, I would know for sure whether I was good enough or not. If I had decided to quit at any stage, I would never have known if I could have made it in the big league.

So, I just kept showing up. It was what I did. I trained hard, and I played well. It was my go-to position. Please don't get me wrong, that doesn't mean there weren't times when I wanted to throw in the towel. I had many thoughts about quitting, numerous tantrums, plenty of attitude attacks, and a disturbing number of thoughts about what I wanted to do to the senior coach. However, my habit was to just keep showing up and working hard, so that's what I did.

The 1985 season rolled around and started the same way, with me sitting on a Thursday night waiting, with hope, to hear my name being called out. The same story! No name, no game, and no fame! So, I did what I always did. I kept showing up. I can't tell you how many times I decided to quit, but something inside me brought me back to training and to the game in the reserve grade team every single time. Finally, that unconscious habit of just showing up finally paid off. After twenty months of rejection, doubt, anger, hopelessness, and despair, that unconscious routine of showing up paid off in many more ways than I first thought.

Firstly, and most obviously, I got selected. Secondly, and what was not so obvious, was the person and footballer I had become in those twenty months. You see, at the time of my first game in 1983, I was not ready to be a senior player. I was not strong enough, fit enough, emotionally intelligent enough, resilient enough, persistent enough, or skilled enough. Those twenty months of what seemed like failure, rejection, and discouragement were the most productive, effective, and memorable of my entire seven-year professional career. The habit I developed eventually got me there when nothing seemed to be working for so long.

The third and greatest benefit is how it has impacted my life ever since. I endured twenty months of rejection, humiliation, and disappointment to create the routine of persistence and showing up. Those twenty months, from August 1983 to April 1985, was a long time ago, and I can tell you this habit has been the one that has helped me most in my life. It has helped me in so many ways. Just to name a few, it helped in my personal training career, in relationships, building muscle when it didn't seem possible, and becoming an author. This amazing trait, I spent all that time creating, has helped me sustain almost seven years to publish *Dance Until It Rains* about my mother's life and cancer journey.

When I decided to write *Dance Until It Rains*, it was September 2004. My mother had survived and thrived for fifteen years longer than her secondary cancer prognosis had predicted. I spent a week with her, talking, asking questions, and telling her how much I loved her. I decided, at that time, I would write a book about her courage and her inspiring journey. Tragically, three months after this decision, she passed away. I was heartbroken and devastated but determined to write the book and get her message, inspiration, and legacy out to the world.

To cut an exceptionally long story short, it took me quite a few years to get over the loss of my mother and finish the manuscript. It took me another two years, many submissions and numerous – more than fifty – rejections from publishers and literary agents to finally find one. It took me another eighteen months to re-write and polish the book before it was finally published at the start of 2011. The book took from September 2004 to January 2011, almost six and half years. So, what kept me going?

I can tell that in all those years, there were many times I felt like giving up, not just on the book but on many things in my life. It was hard at times, as my heart was broken from the loss of my mother. It was often very confusing and incredibly frustrating. There were many times I felt discouraged yet, amidst that, I was hopeful and filled with faith that I would hold the book in my hands. The key to me finally getting a result I will be proud of forever was the routine I had developed as a young footballer, of just getting up and showing up. As I now lift my head and look up from my computer screen to my bookshelf and see, not just *Dance Until it Rains* but all my books, I am smiling. I know I am here, not due to luck, talent, or circumstances. I worked through the discomfort and inconvenience to create powerful unconscious routines with all the simple actions required to be a successful published author.

I want to finish this chapter with one more powerful story. This is a story about Kieren Perkins, the legendary Australian Olympic dual gold medal-winning 1,500 metres swimmer. Kieren talks about his own journey and credits his success to what he refers to as his *worst practised habit*. He is an iconic Australian hero who swam the 1,500 metres event for many years. He swam in three consecutive Olympic Games in 1992, 1996 and 2000. He won two gold medals and one silver medal, and ironically, he was not a swimmer. He was not even very athletic at all. The only reason he started swimming was that, as a child, he ran through a plate glass window, seriously severing tendons in his leg. His rehabilitation program involved months of water therapy. Once rehabilitated, he decided to join the swimming squad at the pool he attended at that time.

He was not a swimmer at all. In fact, at his first swimming carnival, he came dead last by a long way. However, his coach had taught him to focus on individual improvement, stay in his own lane, and not worry about other swimmers. From a young age, he trained to a specific swim plan, and that plan was to go out hard for the first 200 metres, keep a steady pace for 1,200 metres and then push home for the last 100 metres. He practised, trained, and repeated this strategy over many years. He became unconsciously competent with this strategy. As I mentioned, he calls it his *worst practised habit*.

The power of Kieren's unconscious routine was clearly demonstrated at the 1996 Atlanta Olympic Games. He had a poor lead up to the games. He had injuries, was not in great condition, and his form was not at its peak. He was, however, good enough to make it to the semi-finals. In this race, he found himself in an unfamiliar position, behind by a long way and not in a good mental or emotional state. Even as he was swimming in the race, he thought of how bad he was feeling and how embarrassing it would be to make it to the final and then lose. He explained how he decided, while swimming in that semi-final, to deliberately miss out on qualifying for the final. He thought it would be better to avoid the final altogether than make it and not win. So consciously, in his mind, he slowed down. That was until he finished the race, touched the wall, looked up at the scoreboard to see, with surprise and dismay, he had qualified in eighth position. He was accidentally in the final.

From the eighth lane, he went on to win the final and the gold medal with ease. The burning question is, how, while he was going through all that mental and emotional turmoil in the semi-final, was he able to qualify for the final? Simple, his competent unconscious routine, or as he describes it, his *worst practised habit*, took over and guided him to the final and then to the gold medal. He had practised, rehearsed, and repeated his swim strategy for so many years that it was just what he did, irrespective of how he felt. His mind had conditioned his body to deliver that result time after time. Kieren Perkins is an Australian swimming legend today and forever, because of his unconscious habits far more than his ability.

The power twins

As I wrap up this chapter, I need to add one more element to the unconscious competence discussion. It will take some time to get to the point when the actions you want to be *just what you do* become embedded neural pathways in your brain. I will discuss some strategies to make this happen in the next chapter but, for now, I want to let you know that the two key elements that have helped me the most are faith and patience. In his book, *The Force of Faith*, Kenneth Copeland calls faith and patience the *power twins*. He says: *'When faith has a tendency to waver, it is patience to come to faith's aid to make it stand'*. He goes on to say: *'Together they will produce, every time. Patience without faith has no power to call into the reality the things desired because faith is the substance of things hoped for. So, patience without faith has no substance.'*

As I look back, I can see the impact of these *power twins* on every single one of my achievements. There is no doubt that total faith, work, and painful patience, were the key to becoming a regular senior professional footballer. It could only have been faith mixed with its powerful twin, patience, that allowed me to be sitting here today and writing my eighth book. Moving from a skinny body to a more muscular and athletic physique, when it just didn't seem possible, took faith, patience, and work, for it to happen. Before you read the next chapter and start to create unconscious habits from the actions you need to take consistently to achieve your dreams, remember the power twins, faith and patience.

Moving towards 'TEARS of Joy'

Romans 12:2 – *Do not conform to the pattern of this world, but be transformed by the renewing of your mind. Then you will be able to test and approve what God's will is – his good, pleasing and perfect will.* (NIV)

The 'TEARS of joy' you will experience in your life will only come after you have established the right unconscious habits or routines. Luck has nothing to do with it. Make no mistake, my friend. The outcomes in your life, now and forever, will be determined by the routines you establish, whether amazing, good, bad, or ugly. Please don't miss this point. There are many fabulous books I would encourage you to find that talk about the power of simple daily habits. *The Compound Effect* by Darren Hardy is awesome. *The Slight Edge* by Jeff Olsen is amazing. I am currently reading a book called *Atomic Habits* by James Clear, which I am loving.

In the next chapter, I talk more about creating these wonderful life-transforming routines, but right now I want you to really think hard and be honest with yourself. Think about things you are excelling in your life, and reflect on the thinking and routines in these areas. Now for the tough part, think about the areas you are not happy with, and do the same. Be honest, take responsibility for your actions, and determine what you would need to change to create rituals that will transform that area of your life.

I have given you quite a few examples of the power of routine, and the mistake you may make is thinking that success is available to others but not to you. Again I will say that success is NOT the result of talent, age, connections, education, money, time, circumstances, or luck. Instead, every seemingly spectacular success is the simple culmination of many simple, daily, and less than spectacular actions that have been focused on, and developed into, unconscious routines. The moment you realise this, believe it, and start acting on it, is the moment you will not be able to sleep because of excitement. Then things will start to change in your life.

Key questions and action steps

1. Now, time to be totally honest with yourself. Think about the areas you are stuck in or failing at. Can you identify the thinking and unconscious competence you have developed around that area of life?

2. Can you see, logically and predictably, why you are not fulfilling your destiny in that area of life?

3. Why do you think that is? Be honest here. If you want things to change, is it your thinking and habits that need to change?

4. Now examine one area of life in which you are flourishing. What are the habits or routines you have in this area?

5. Why do you think you have developed great habits in this area instead of the areas you are struggling in?

6. Are you ready to make some change to create the unconscious competence that will give you everything you want?

7. Are you willing to apply faith and patience to this process?

8. If yes, keep reading.

CHAPTER 13

Developing success routines

"It only takes 63 days to create a strong, unbreakable
neural pathway in the brain. In other words, a
routine that will enhance your life forever."

There is no doubt about it. I am a creature of habit. My routines are so firmly established that I find it difficult to stray from them for even one day. This can cause me some angst at times but, nevertheless, I am incredibly grateful for these routines. Why? Because I am very clear, the things I have achieved, the life I live today, and the life I will live in the future are 100 per cent determined by my routines. To start this chapter, I want to share my morning routine, which is what sets up each day and the successes I enjoy. I am not sharing this to impress you but to impress upon you the power of routine. Once I describe what I do, I will explain how I have been able to do it.

My alarm is set for 5:15 am, but rarely does it go off because I am awake at 5:10 am, ready to rock before it activates. Without even being conscious of what I am doing, I get up, put my training gear on, drink one litre of purified water, eat a small protein-based snack, and am out the door to do my exercise. It's important to note here I don't love exercise, nor do I often even feel like it, so why is it that I never miss a morning? I am so grateful it is now an unconscious routine, and I always love it when it is over. After exercise, I spend time in prayer and meditation. Then I drink more water, eat some fruit and protein, eat my first lot of organic plant-based vitamin supplements, and then take my dog Joia for her walk.

I have already mentioned that, while walking Joia, I listen to and sing along with worship songs, and I jog on the spot while she stops to pee, poo, and sniff, so I maximise my step count. When I get back from this walk, I eat more healthy food. I sit down to read and write out my affirmations, goals, strengths, and gratitude list. I then turn on my computer, check and respond to my emails and messages from overnight. I then track my income and expenses and fill in my financial spreadsheets. Next, I get onto LinkedIn, respond to messages, and search potential contacts, then send out twenty messages to twenty new people to potentially connect and collaborate with.

I hope I am not boring you! By this time, it's about 7:45 am and, at this time every day, Monday to Friday, I call my mentor and check in with him. We talk for ten to fifteen minutes, and it helps keep me accountable and on track. My next task is writing more of my next book, editing my next podcast, and putting some thoughts into my blog for the week. By this time, it's okay to start calling people. So, I spend about an hour making calls to set up meetings, introduce myself to potential clients and follow up connections I have already made.

By this time, it's about 10:00 am, and I have set up my day and my week, and I feel amazing. The rest of the day, I have the flexibility to have meetings, present talks, do podcast interviews, write more, spend time with friends and family, walk Joia again, have a power nap if I want, or do anything else I choose to do. By the end of the day, I have easily done 10,000 steps, I have achieved a lot, I feel amazing, and I always sleep like a champion. Before you conclude I am a robot, I just need to say here

I do have off days and challenges. However, my rituals really help me negotiate and deal with almost anything that comes my way.

You may be thinking that all sounds very demanding, overwhelming, and extreme, but let me tell you, it's actually a piece of cake. Why? Simply because these tasks are no longer things I need to worry about, stress about, decide about, negotiate or debate about, they are now just what I automatically do. They are embedded in my psyche and part of my DNA. How cool is that?

In different areas of life, I often get asked if I believe we need to focus every day on the important things. To be optimally healthy, do we need to focus every day on eating well, exercise, drinking water, and other healthy actions? To be a successful author, do we need to focus every day on writing, editing, submitting, or promoting? To have great relationships, do we need to focus every day on the things that will build them? To be financially stable, do we need to focus every day on earning and saving? How would you answer any of these questions? You may be surprised at the answer I give.

My answer is no, we should not have to focus every day on the most important things. Does that sound weird? Does it sound like a contradiction? Well, here is my thinking, if we need to focus every day on the important actions, they are not yet unconscious routines. Do we need to focus on them for a period? Absolutely we do, although the end goal should be not to need to focus on healthy eating, regular exercise, writing your book, building relationships, saving money, or any other of the most important things in your life. The goal should be to turn them into unconscious routines so that, like my morning routine, they are embedded in your psyche and part of your DNA. I no longer need to focus on these things anymore. This chapter is all about helping you achieve the same wonderful position.

By now, I am sure you understand our lives are driven and determined by our routines. All the outcomes we experience in life are the direct result of these routines. Yes, I said all. Not some, not most, but all. I hope I have been able to make that point loud and clear in the last chapter. You may believe some outcomes are out of your control and not the result of routine. If so, I urge you to think deeply, not just about the circumstances that may well be out of your control, but the way you react to and handle those situations. It is the reaction to the circumstance, not the circumstance itself, that will determine the outcomes in your life. This reaction is a habit or routine for you, just as it is for me.

When my professional football career was cut short, I truly believed it was the event of being sacked that was out of my control and unfair. Let me tell you now, the end of my professional career had nothing to do with that event. It had everything to do with my declining attitude and poor routines leading up to the sacking, and my irresponsible reaction to the event after it happened. Both causes were the routines I had developed to an unconscious competence in my life. Just like Kieren Perkins' *worst practised habit* took him to the top of the sport of swimming, mine at the time took me out the other end. If you were to really reflect on your life, the outcomes you have and will experience, and are brutally honest with yourself, you will know that your routines are the cause. It is not luck or out-of-your-control circumstances.

I have previously talked about my mother and how she turned a horrendous diagnosis and two-year death sentence into a fifteen-year journey of joy, gratitude, and blessings. I passionately believe the reason she lived for an additional fourteen years when her secondary liver cancer was diagnosed, was not luck, medication, or genetics. It was because of the many positive unconscious routines she developed for herself.

First and foremost, my mother knew she had to focus on her purpose and what was most important to her every day. This thinking and focus moved her into a more positive emotional state, which led her to initiate many actions that became life-giving and joy-producing habits. Things like: meditation; affirmation; gratitude lists; forgiveness; juicing; eating better quality foods; daily movement; supplementation; journaling; and many other things. It is no wonder – to me anyway – why, in her situation, she could add those extra years and quality living to her life. It was just tragic that she didn't start to create these wonderful routines earlier in her life. Maybe she would still be here.

My point is, no matter how bad it may seem, we can take any situation and turn it into a positive experience. This can be done by developing the right routines and creating unconscious competence. I have mentioned this a few times, so let's look at it in a little more detail. There is a process to get to the point of wonderfully developed unconscious rituals, as you will know if you ever tried to change them. It's hard! It takes time, focus, discomfort, and strong resistance to the natural pull back to your old ways. The goal is always to get to unconscious competence, but we all start at unconscious incompetence. The diagram below has come from a wonderful article called *'The four stages of competence'* written by Zainab Zaki on www.medium.com.

UNCONSCIOUS INCOMPETENCE
You are unaware of the skill and your lack of proficiency

UNCONSCIOUS COMPETENCE
Performing the skill becomes automatic

CONSCIOUS INCOMPETENCE
You are aware of the skill but not yet proficient

CONSCIOUS COMPETENCE
You are able to use the skill, but only with effort

As I try to explain this process to you, I will use a personal example to help you understand it, how it is happening, and how it can be applied in your life.

As you may have gathered so far, I have always been ambitious and hard-working. This is something that had been drilled into me from a young age. I always thought if you worked hard enough, and for long enough, you could achieve anything you wanted, so that's what I did. After fifteen years of personal training, I got to the point when I worked ridiculously hard in two businesses, my personal training business, and a café. My thinking was this would give me the significance and financial success I was after. I was wrong because I was **unconsciously incompetent**. In other words, I didn't know what I didn't know. I was unaware, at the time, that just working hard was not enough. I also needed to work smart.

I got to the stage when I knew what I was doing wasn't getting me where I wanted to be. Working seven days a week and being almost $100,000 in debt is a pretty good indicator! I just wasn't sure how to get out of this situation and create the life I wanted. At the time, a friend of mine lent me a book called '*Rich Dad, Poor Dad*' by Robert Kiyosaki. As I read the book, my jaw dropped as, suddenly, I had a chilling realisation about how wrong I had been in my attempts at creating financial success. I'm not sure if you've read the book, but he talks about financial intelligence, of which, at the time, I had zero! The message I got from the book was loud and clear, if you continue to just trade time for money, which is what I was doing, you will always work. That initially discouraged me. He then went on to say the only way to create financial options and freedom is through diversification and building assets that are income producing. It sounded great, but I had no idea how to do it. I had, at that moment, become **consciously incompetent**. In other words, I knew what I needed to do. I just didn't how to do it.

This was an incredibly exciting and frustrating time of my life. I'm not sure if you know what I mean. On the one hand, I had discovered what I had been doing wrong for all my working life, and I had found out there was another way, which was exciting. On the other hand, I had no idea what to do, where to start, or whether I could do it, which was frustrating. My idea of income-producing assets required large capital investment, and I had no capital to invest. In fact, I was paying off the massive debt I incurred when my café failed spectacularly. So, I was feeling a little helpless in my conscious incompetence. On the positive side, I always believe I can find a way to get things done. So, I kept reading more of Robert Kiyosaki's books, with my radar on and ready to find the solution that would work for me.

Just a few days later, with my intention clear, God intervened. At the time, I didn't recognise it as divine intervention. I thought it was coincidental or Universal. It was incredible. For whatever reason, I was introduced to an eCommerce business idea that didn't require a large capital outlay and could generate this asset style income. To say I was excited was an understatement but also a little fearful and sceptical. I was largely ignorant, and for no logical reason, I was very arrogant. I was, however, not stupid, and I thought: *What's the worst that could happen if I give it a go for a few months and test the waters?* So that's what I did. I got started in an industry that was totally foreign to me, so I had to focus and learn very deliberately to develop the skills I needed. I then moved into the stage of **conscious competence**. In other words, I was starting to develop the skills I needed, and I began getting positive results. However, it still took deliberate and conscious focus, effort, and attention.

As I worked away in this new business for a couple of months, positive results were happening. I could see this being the vehicle to help me retire from personal training to follow my purpose and passion of being a full-time speaker and author. As I'm sure you can imagine, this excited me. I kept working, kept repeating the skills, and continued to experience positive results. In fact, within the first twelve months, I had developed an asset-based income that allowed me to more than half my personal training hours and be retired in two years.

Within those two years, with daily focus and attention to simple actions, for a relatively short period of time, I became unconsciously competent. In other words, I was doing the things I needed to do to create an ongoing result automatically. These simple actions had become powerful unconscious routines. As I write this, that was more than fifteen years ago. The unconscious mindset I developed and the ongoing money I created has been flowing in continuously ever since. That is the power of taking the time to become **unconsciously competent** or, in lay terms, create great unconscious routines!

Whether you are deliberate about it, focus on it, or not, you are creating routines and habits, every second, every minute, every hour, of every day. Most of us mistakenly believe each thought or perspective we focus on, the emotion we experience, and the action we take are isolated events and not a big deal. Wow, that is a serious and monumental error! Every action, no matter how small and insignificant it seems, is a very big deal. Why? Because it started with a thought that led to an emotion, which initiated the action which will, over time, develop a routine. There is no such thing as an isolated event. Everything is connected, and every thought, emotion, and action will ripple out to create routines and outcomes in your life and in many other lives. So, be very deliberate about your thoughts, emotions, and actions.

No one wants to struggle financially, but many find themselves in financial deficit because, without deliberate focus, they fall into routines that lead to this outcome. I don't meet anyone who declares that poor health is what they are after. Yet, a disturbing number of people around the globe, without paying attention, develop habits leading to disease and poor health. I know of no one who, standing at the altar of their wedding, is thinking about divorce. However the rates are dramatic, as thoughtless and unconsidered relationship habits developed, leading people to just that. I know this from personal and painful experiences. The most important thing to realise is while the habit or routine will lead to the outcome, it all starts with the thought, belief, or perspective we focus on. It's either focused and deliberate or a thought that we simply allow into our head and stay. Can you see why every thought is so critical?

Understanding our routine formation

Anthony Robbins, speaker and motivator, talks about the reason why we do <u>all</u> things. He states every action we take is to avoid pain or gain pleasure. That's it. It is no more complicated than that. Our initial instinct is often to avoid short-term pain, and/or gain short-term pleasure. When we do this, we often don't consider the long-term consequence of the action we take. Right now, I will encourage you to seriously consider the long-term consequences of the routine that will be developed by the short-term action you take. You see, so very often, short-term pleasure will lead to long-term pain and, on the flip side, short-term pain can very well lead to long-term pleasure.

Let me tell you about a famous experiment. Author Daniel Goldman writes about this well-known study conducted by researchers at Stanford University. It is the most celebrated example showing the phenomenon of delayed gratification and patience. It is now what has become popularly known in professional circles as the ***Marshmallow Test***. This is what he said:

> A four-year-old child is put in a room with a plate containing one marshmallow and is told that the experimenter must run an errand. If the four-year-old can wait until the experimenter returns, then they can have

two marshmallows. If they want to eat now, they can certainly do that but will only get one marshmallow.

The experiment highlights the eternal battle between impulse and restraint, desire and control and gratification and delay. The children employed all kinds of strategies to wait for, and receive, the extra marshmallow. They would sit on their hands, sing themselves songs, tell themselves stories, play with their fingers and sniff the marshmallow. One child even bent down and began to lick the table as if the flavour had somehow morphed into the wood!

This simple experiment showed the impact this one-character trait, displayed at the age of four, had on the lives of those who took part in the experiment. The research team tracked these children for many years. Those who were able to wait, as four-year-old's, grew up to be more socially competent, better able to cope with stress and less likely to give up under pressure than those who could not wait.

The *marshmallow grabbers* grew up to be more stubborn and indecisive, more easily upset by frustration and more resentful about not getting enough. Most amazingly, the group of *marshmallow waiters* had SAT (USA achievement) scores that averaged 210 points higher than the group of *marshmallow grabbers*. Moreover, the *marshmallow grabbers* were still unable to put off gratification all those years later.

The studies have shown that poor impulse control is more likely to be associated with delinquency, substance abuse and divorce. No wonder the author, in summarising this study, calls the **ability to wait well** *the master aptitude*. He also suggests the inability to control impulses, the refusal to live in patient waiting and trust lies close to the heart of human nature. It has been that way ever since Adam and Eve took a bite from the forbidden *marshmallow*!

As you can see from the ***Marshmallow Test***, the routine of being tempted and seduced by the gain of immediate pleasure can lead to many undesirable situations in life. I'm sure you, like me, have experienced this in your lives to this stage. When we can resist the immediate pleasure and go through some short-term pain, like waiting, persisting, growing, and struggling, the pleasure on the other side is far more fulfilling and gratifying. This is what happens when we spend the time to create the right routines in our lives.

When we fall for the short-term pleasure trap, it can become a devastating long-term routine in life, as the study illustrated so powerfully. Four-year-old children who started down the quick-fix, marshmallow-grabbing mindset path continued to have difficulties at school, at university, in their careers, and with their relationships. So, as you are now thinking about the process of creating the routines in your life that will truly lead to 'TEARS of joy', this understanding of the pleasure-pain principle is critical.

Suppose the reason we act is to gain pleasure or avoid pain. We can choose to chase short-term pleasure that will lead to long-term pain or short-term pain, leading to long-term pleasure. Assuming we want long-term pleasure, the question is: how do we develop the mental and emotional strength to help us resist the quick fix that fixes nothing? In other words, how do you become the person who embraces short-term discomfort and delayed gratification to create routines leading to the life you want and 'TEARS of joy'?

Developing the ability to wait

The great saying passed down through generations is *patience is a virtue*. I know it, you know it. In fact, we all know it. The question is, do we believe it and are we living it? Well, the evidence all around the world suggests this is not the case. So many people are sick, struggling financially, and have conflict and relationship challenges because they are just hoping that chasing quick-fix solutions and short-term pleasure will give them the results they want.

The first step of this process is awareness. For much of my life, I have chased quick fixes, instant gratification, and short-term pleasure. I was not a very patient person. We now live in a microwave, quick-fix, and immediate-answer-society where it is sold to us that everything is available at the click of a button. The devastating problem with this is that a purposeful life of joyful longevity is not available at the click of a button. At the end of the last chapter, I said it will take faith and patience to create the routines that will last. So here are two questions I would like to pose to you. Are you patient or impatient? Would you eat the one marshmallow or wait for the reward of two? If you want the life you want, you need to have an honest awareness and appraisal of your current tendencies.

If you have been seduced into finding quick-fix answers and are now serious about wanting to be a *marshmallow waiter*, there is work to do. Are you ready for it and up for it? If you answer yes, I will outline ideas and strategies to employ, starting when? Tomorrow, next week when you feel like it, or right now? You know the answer to that one. If you want the results and are ready to go, stop making excuses, stop procrastinating, and stop looking for a click-of-a-button option. Let's get started today. That's not too harsh, is it? Even if it is, I don't apologise. It's your life we are talking about. Let's get into this exciting adventure.

Not willpower, why-power

For most people, including me, I think the greatest resistance to change and to create long-term, marshmallow-waiting, and unconsciously competent routines is the horribly incorrect perception that it will be hard and require massive willpower. People who are not clear on what they want are not emotionally compelled to create change and will find it difficult to stick to a process and achieve unconscious competence. They will often suggest it's because they don't have enough willpower. The reality is, they are not clear on their why. Therefore the key first step in the routine forming process is fuelling your why-power!

I've already spoken about this, *ad-nauseam*. Unless you are clear about what is important in your life, and why a change will help you fulfil your purpose, you will need to rely on that elusive willpower. So many people join a gym, but so few use it to get the results they want. The few successful people have an emotionally compelling reason. A reason far greater than a six-pack, buns of steel, or getting into the bikini for a holiday. They are doing it to be an example to their children. They are doing it to be a better parent, boss, or friend. They attend the gym to give them the health and energy required to build their foundation, community, career, or business. They have a purpose far greater than large biceps and tight buns! Most people, who don't get the results they want, believe willpower is required and that they don't have what it takes.

When you know what you want and why, willpower is no longer necessary. You will have a purpose, a strong focus, discover a compelling desire, and be unstoppable. When this happens your resilience simply rises to the surface, as we all have these strengths and traits within us.

This is the only reason a skinny, sickly, and struggling teenager could endure the physical and emotional challenges to be a professional footballer. It wasn't because I had willpower, that's for sure. It was because the vision I had of running onto the ground in front of thousands of screaming fans and feeling admiration, gave me the why-power without ever negotiating the price.

If my mother was alive today, she would not have credited her remarkable, against-all-odds, surviving and thriving for fifteen years to willpower. She identified her purpose, discovered there were faces attached to it, and she found her why. She just automatically engaged in action mode from that moment, and she did what she had to do. While she didn't always love it, she never again questioned it or told herself it was too hard. Her why was that powerful. As is yours. The first and most important step in creating the routines that will take you to wherever you want to go is to know where you want to go and why!

Only 63 days

It was ironic, coincidence, or divinely orchestrated, that I became aware of the truth about how long it takes to form a strong, firmly embedded, and unconsciously competent routine. I was always under the impression it took 21 days to create a habit. You? The problem was, as I believed this to be true, I thought there must be something wrong with me. Why? Because no matter how hard I tried, I could never develop a habit in 21 days that would stick. I thought maybe my brain is different to most. Maybe I'm a bit thicker because of all the times I got beaten around the head as a footballer.

Just as I believed I was different, weird, and broken, I attended an inspirational conference where Keith Abraham, a very successful businessman and author, was a speaker. He introduced the idea that it takes 63 days to create this unbreakable chemical change and powerful routine. He explained the first 21 days start forming the habit. The second 21 days strengthen it, so the old habit doesn't overpower it. The final 21-days embed it and make it part of DNA, forever.

Now this made sense to me, but how was I to know it wasn't just a Keith Abraham's good idea? I mean, clearly, the 21-day habit thing was obviously someone else's idea, as it had no evidence in science to back it up. Then soon after, and totally from an unrelated source, I was introduced to Dr Caroline Leaf. She is a cognitive neuroscientist who has spent the last thirty years researching the mind-brain connection, the nature of mental health, and the formation of memory. She was one of the first to study how the brain can change with directed mind input (neuroplasticity). In her clinical practice, she helped thousands of people use their minds to detox and use their brain to succeed in life, including school, university, and the workplace.

The next excerpts are taken from a blog on her website www.drleaf. com, called 'Why we keep making the same mistakes and tips to break bad habits':

> Indubitably, it is easier to just keep reacting the way we usually react. An automated behaviour is just that, automatic, and as such requires far less mental energy because it is entrenched in our nonconscious mind, which is very influential in future decision-making. Indeed, it is generally more comfortable to act or speak in ways we are familiar with, even if the results of our mistakes cause us pain or discomfort.

> Change can, of course, also be uncomfortable. To overcome this pain, we must **want** to change. This may sound redundant, but when it comes to making the same mistakes, you must ask yourself if you really, truly

want to change and are willing to work hard and face yourself. Do your reactions and the impact they have on others concern you enough to go through the process of change? Are you willing to put in the time and mental effort to change? Are you desperate enough to stop making the same mistakes repeatedly?

As they say, Rome wasn't built in a day. It takes time to change, so give yourself a break if you do make a mistake or fail! Trying to change yourself too fast can cause unnecessary stress, making you more anxious and setting you up for what I call the "shame spiral" because you feel like you keep failing and are not able to change. But it takes a minimum of 63 days to change an automated habit – when it comes to the mind, there really are no quick fixes, and most people give up on day four, so be patient!

So as you can now see, from a neuroscience point of view, it takes at least 63 days to create a strong neural pathway in the brain. It will be good or bad, enhancing, or destructive, based on how deliberate you are about its formation. When deliberately and positively created, this solid and unbreakable habit will change your life for the better forever, even if it's just one single and simple thing.

Several years I spoke at a law firm to a group of very analytical lawyers about improving their wellbeing. I outlined seven very simple daily behaviours that would have an incredible effect on their lives if they were developed into habits. Most of them didn't believe me. After the talk, one lady came to me and said she was too busy to try and include all seven but would simply start drinking an extra 500ml of water per day.

Who could have possibly imagined what this seemingly insignificant daily habit could do? Indeed, not this lady.

I returned to the firm three months later to be enthusiastically greeted by someone who looked familiar, but I couldn't quite recognise. After a few minutes, I realised it was the lady who had committed to the extra 500ml of water per day. Wow, did she look different?! When I first met her, she was pale, had dark circles under her eyes, was a little chubby and very lethargic. As I stood in front of her just three months later, I looked at a very different person. She bounced, she beamed, her skin looked amazing, no more bags under her eyes, and she had lost weight. *Surely not just from drinking 500ml of water each day?*

Not directly, but indirectly, yes, it was from just that one simple decision. She explained she really wanted to feel better and have more quality time with her kids. Hence, she focused on making drinking additional water an *unconsciously competent* routine in her life. Then, without even knowing what she was doing, she unlocked a powerful belief in herself. She deliberately drank water every day and created a strong neural pathway in her brain. Because this one daily action helped her feel better, she was motivated to add other daily habits, like eating breakfast, walking, and drinking less coffee. Initially, she believed she could only change one thing. The result was the ripple effect that transformed her life, her family, and the people in her office.

So, as you can see from this example, you only need to make one or two minor changes in your daily habit patterns. It will have an incredible flow-on effect in your life, and many other lives that you may not even realise. Just 63 days of focus is all it takes. It sounds like a lot, but really, when you reflect, it's such a tiny percentage and investment of your life for such a life-changing payoff. Is it worth it? If it is, I have a tool to help. It's a simple 63-day tracking sheet, and here is how to use it to change your life:

Step one – Print off the *63-day tracking sheet* from https://andrewjobling.com.au/resources-downloads/.

Step two – Set a goal to create some focus and a specific destination. Pick an area of your life to focus on. Then think about what you would like to achieve in that area of your life. Then, using the format at the top of the sheet, visualise it, feel it and then write it. Here is an example for you:

It is 15 September 2021. I feel excited, proud, and on purpose as I hold my eighth published book, 'TEARS of joy', in my hands. I have rewarded myself with a celebratory meal out with important people in my life.

The key aspects of this goal-setting process are:

1. It is written in the present tense as if it has already happened. This is important because anything you focus on, or affirm in the future, will stay there.
2. The date is set, and the goal is specific, significant, and achievable.
3. The emotion is visualised, experienced, and expressed to drive the action.
4. A reward is attached to further add fuel to its achievement. There is something special about the reward after the achievement of a goal. You will enjoy it so much more than just doing it anyway.
5. Read the goal and visualise it every day.

Step three – Write in the section underneath the stated goal, why its achievement is important to you.

Step four – Select one, two and no more than three simple daily actions you would like to turn into unconscious routines and write them in as A1 – A3. Please note, it is better start with just one and nail it rather than try too many and feel overwhelmed. I have seen it happen many times.

Step five – Every single day, for 63 days, whether you feel like it or not, read the goal, focus on your why, act, tick the box, win the day, and celebrate doing it.

Step six – Before you start, and throughout the 63 days, repeat this affirmation to yourself or something similar – *'I am a winner. I easily stick to my 63-day plan, one day at a time. I take the actions, tick the boxes, and win every single day. I am becoming the person I have always wanted to be.'*

Make no mistake, just 63 days is all it takes to create, develop, strengthen, and embed an unconscious behaviour pattern that will transform your life. You would not be reading this book if not for this transformational process in my life. Could you focus and win every day for 63 days? Is it worth it? It will take focus, it may be uncomfortable, there will be times when you don't want to, or couldn't be bothered. Do it anyway! You may be asking: *Is it okay if I miss a day here or there?* That's a valid question, and I want to answer it using an analogy.

If you have travelled by plane, you would expect the pilot to taxi to the start of the runway, accelerate until the plane had enough speed to take off before the runway ended. Are you with me here? What would happen if, at any time during the acceleration period, the pilot hits the brakes and slows the plane down, even for a few seconds? Would they be able to get it back up to the necessary speed to take off before the runway ends? Just in case you are wondering, the answer to that question is no! If the pilot does accelerate, then brake and try to accelerate again, the plane will not get enough speed up for take-off. It will either crash off the end of the runway or go all the way back to the start and try again.

I hope you're getting my drift here. If you miss a day in your 63-day process, it's just like hitting the brakes on take-off, even just for a split second. Remember, we are trying to create a new mindset here. Allowing yourself to miss a day is a decision you make in your mind that will potentially lead to the wrong neural pathway being created. It's just as easy to do it as it is to not. So, focus and act <u>every</u> single day for 63 days. Remember to win the day. If you do miss a day, it's okay, don't beat yourself up. Just print off a new tracking sheet and start again.

Win the day

I have referred to *win the day* a few times already in this chapter and this book. I want to make sure you really understand the power of this concept and how it is the most important one to help you get to the end of the runway with enough speed to take off. In other words, make it through 63 days without missing one. I don't know about you, but I cannot focus on something for 63 days. There are too many potential distractions that I know will come along and knock me off track. I can't focus for 42 days, 21 days or even seven days. For me, it's too hard and too overwhelming.

What I can do is focus on one day. That day is today! If all I must think about is today, then I am in control. I don't know what will happen tomorrow, next week or next month, but I can make today count. So, in my journey of creating the routines I have in my life, I focus on the only day I have, and the only day that matters. That is today. I am a box ticker, and I love it. Every time I act and tick a box, I feel like a winner, and inside I do a celebratory happy dance. For example, when it comes to exercise, all I think about is the moment I have finished what I must do. I get the job done, win the day, and then celebrate. I do this and have done this with each seemingly insignificant action I want to develop into a strong unbreakable neural pathway in my brain.

You will not create these unconscious habits in a day, but you will do it day by day. It's so much easier to think about and focus on just today. Make a big deal of today, the action you take, and the box you tick. Too many people think that success comes after you tick the box on the 63rd day. Wrong! Success happens today when you take the step, do what you've set yourself to do, and you tick the box. If you don't focus on winning each day, and you continually look at how far you must go, you will not get to day 63 to celebrate. So do it every single day on the journey. Just win today and then, when midnight strikes, guess what happens? You have a new today to win.

The power of accountability, support, and community

A study was done using two groups of people who were in very bad physical shape. Because of their ailing health, both groups had been told by doctors if they didn't make changes to their eating and their lifestyle, they would not survive for much longer. Wow, you couldn't get much more incentive to change than that. The first group was given this news by doctors and were sent off with an action plan of things they needed to change to save their lives. Guess what percentage of these people, even with the risk of imminent death, stuck to, made the necessary changes, and created new positive routines in their lives? Incredibly, only one out of ten! Nine out of ten people, knowing that if they didn't change, they would die, said to themselves something like: *Oh well, I guess my time is up. It's too hard to change now!* That is mind-blowing to me.

The second group of people were given the same news by doctors and sent off with an action plan of things they needed to change to save their lives. The difference was that the individuals in this group had an accountability partner. They had someone they needed to check in with regularly to see how they were going. They had someone who would help, encourage, and support them through this challenging period of their lives. From this second group of people, eight out of ten stuck to making the necessary changes and created new positive routines in their lives. This is the power of accountability, support, and community.

The other experiment to even further reinforce the need for encouragement and accountability was the *'standing in iced water'* test. Subjects were asked to stand in icy cold water, in a room on their own, isolated from other human contact, for as long as they could. I can't remember the exact length of time the average person could tolerate the discomfort. However, I do know that things dramatically changed when they added support and encouragement. When there was someone with them in the room, encouraging them, they could tolerate the freezing cold and last for more than twice as long.

The message here is a simple one, don't try to do this alone. Getting through 63 days of creating long-term, deeply embedded routines in your life will be a tough ask if attempting to do it alone. Please take this next statement the way it's intended, with a deep concern for your wellbeing and life. You need another mind and brain to help you, other than your own. Why? You, like me, have got to the place where you have decided you need to change with your own brain and your own thinking. Trying to create change with that same brain can be a challenge, and oh boy, do I know it! Albert Einstein said: *'We cannot solve our problems with the same thinking we used when we created them'*. Einstein's other well-known quote is: *'Insanity is doing the same thing over and over and expecting a different result'*. Another person's perspective, support, and encouragement can make all the difference.

So find an accountability partner, someone to go on the journey with. Someone to check in with, to be a cheerleader for you, support and encourage you, and not let you off the hook when you feel yourself being pulled back into old habits. It could be your partner, a friend, a mentor, or a coach. Pay someone if you need to, for a short time. This is you and your life I am talking about. You are worth the investment of time, effort, and money to create the change that will totally transform your life.

Could I have played professional football without the support of my family, the help of my junior coaches, the direction of the coaching staff, or the encouragement of my teammates? No way in the world. Could I have possibly become a full-time author without the support and encouragement of the right people, the direction of editors, the public relations team at the publishing house, or the people who bought my books? Not a chance. Your ego may suggest you can do it alone. However, you will need accountability, support, and a strong community to achieve what you want. When you find it, you will start to fly to places you never even dreamed possible. Sir Isaac Newton said: *'If I have seen further than others, it is by standing upon the shoulders of giants'.*

Detox your mind

As you already know, everything you do and have in life, and will do and have in the future, starts with a thought, belief, or perspective you choose to focus on. That being the case, isn't it sensible to detox, protect, nurture, develop and expand our minds if we want to live a purposeful life of joyful longevity? In the process of creating new unconscious routines and habits, your greatest potential enemy is you and your current thinking. Why? Because if your current thinking has got you into the routines that have brought you to read this book, then it would be crazy to think the same thinking could give you a different outcome. Right?

I'm going to assume that you are serious about navigating through the 63 days to create life-enhancing neural pathways in your brain and new powerful permanent routines. Therefore daily attention to detoxing your mind is a must. Yes, I said a must because the world you live in will pollute your thinking if you are not deliberate. The only way to overpower and overcome the world's negativity on your valuable and vulnerable mind is by deliberately putting great stuff in every day.

I know I have spoken about this already, however if staying strong in the 63-day process is important to you, then you must pay daily attention to the following areas:

1. **The people you associate with.** The people you spend most of your time with will significantly impact the life you will live. Are they uplifting, positive, encouraging, and supportive? Do they stretch you to be better and have more? Conversely, are they negative, complaining, critical and toxic? Do they bring you down rather than lift you up? What are their habits? Are they the habits you want for your life? If they are, then you are in the right place. Stay there. If not, can I suggest you get out of there as fast as you can. There have been studies done on the impact of attitude on DNA. DNA strands were placed in Petri dishes and passed between people with different attitudes about life. The impact on these DNA strands was observable, obvious, and immediate. When being held by a negative person, the strands shrivelled in front of the researcher's eyes. The same DNA strands lengthened and plumped up when held by happy and positive people. This means that negative people will damage your DNA and shorten your life. In contrast, positive people will help you live a longer and happier life.

2. **The things you are reading.** When you read, you are significantly affecting your mindset. When you read, you immediately

and powerfully transform your self-talk through the words on the page of whatever you are reading, and deposit them into your mind. So the things you read are important for keeping you on track to creating the habits that will enhance your life experience. Can I suggest a simple routine of just ten to fifteen minutes per day of reading books, blogs, articles, and information? This will inspire, empower, educate, uplift, and reinforce what you are doing? This will absolutely help you stay on track through your 63-day journey. At the same time, for your own sake, read less newspapers, trashy mags and novels with crime, violence, and other content that will pollute your precious mind.

3. **The stuff you watch and listen to.** Everything you listen to will be filtered by your brain and impact your mind. Even things you are unaware of may be playing in the background, or you are not focusing on, like music, conversations, radio, and television. Day after day of listening and taking in these messages will impact your thinking and your life. Listen to positive audios and podcasts while driving. Listen to music that is positive and uplifting. Watch TV shows that make you feel good. As you attempt to create the routines that will change your life, please limit listening to and watching the news, current affairs, crime, and negatively oriented programs.

I'm excited about the routines I have in my life and the results they predictably deliver. I am also very aware of the ones that are not serving me the way I want. In the last chapter, I mentioned the daily routine I created in 2017, and you are reading the result of that routine right now. I have been writing books since 2002, when I began the journey with *Eat Chocolate, Drink Alcohol and be Lean & Healthy.* After that book was published, I became spasmodic with my writing, and did it only when

I felt like it, was inspired or motivated. So, as I'm sure you had already found out in your own life, that's not a lot of writing, even though I thought I was doing much more. I spent so much time thinking about it, I kidded myself I was doing more than I was.

Then, I began mentoring aspiring authors and continually telling them the importance of a daily writing routine. The problem was, at that time, I was not walking the talk. I was writing a little here and there, but certainly not every day, as I was advising my clients to do. So with integrity, and wanting to lead by example in my mind, I set myself the goal of writing every single day for the whole 2017 year. There were certainly days I didn't feel like writing, but I did it anyway. The thing that made me do it was the accountability of knowing I would be talking to a client that day and telling them the importance of writing every day. I had now trapped myself into success because I couldn't talk it if I didn't walk it.

After around 63 days, and I don't exactly know because I didn't count, I was in a rhythm and a flow. Nothing was ever going to stop me from writing every day, ever again. By the end of 2017, with the very conservative target of 500 words per day as I mentioned, I had written almost 200,000 words for the entire year. I have written every day ever since, and will do it forever. Why? Not because I always feel like it. Not because I am always motivated or inspired. Not because I even always enjoy it. I do it because it is now part of my DNA. It is who I am and what I do, no more doubts, fears, or negotiations. This is the power of routine in your life.

Moving towards 'TEARS of Joy'

> 2 Timothy 1:7 – *For the spirit God gave us does not make us timid, but gives us power, love, and self-discipline.* (NIV)

The 'TEARS of joy' you will experience in your life will <u>only</u> come after you have established the right routines. This process is the most challenging you will encounter on your journey to living your best life. Moving from unconscious incompetence to unconscious competence, in certain areas, over a very focused period of at least 63 days, will be the most fulfilling yet testing of your life. Fulfilling because the result is an amazing long-term chemical change in you, your results, and your life. Testing, because you will be tested every day by your own thinking, external circumstances, and other people's opinions.

I mentioned the term *chemical change* in the previous paragraph. What does that mean? It means something that is changed forever. Under intense heat and pressure for millions of years, a common and worthless lump of coal will become a rare and valuable diamond. That is a chemical change as it will never go back to coal again.

Many people don't have the vision, patience, or perseverance to stay the distance to create chemical change. Many want a quick fix, which leads only to a physical change. This would be like putting water in an ice tray and placing it in the freezer. In about an hour that water has frozen and become a solid, right? This is not a permanent chemical change because what happens if you take it and leave it out of the freezer? It returns to the water.

It's like people who go on a diet to lose weight but, in most cases, put the weight back on. It's like many people who win the lottery then lose all that money. They temporarily changed some actions, but they didn't take the time to permanently change their mindset and routines.

The great news is that your positive and powerful chemical change does not need to take millions of years, but it will take more than an hour! In fact it will take at least 63 days, just one day at a time. Utilise one or more of the strategies I have outlined in this chapter to make this work for you. Then the last part, the routine forming part, in the process of achieving the 'TEARS of joy' you are aspiring to, is done. The success you want will then just predictably take care of itself and flow into your life.

Key questions and action steps

1. The most important question I can ask is: are you ready to take this journey and focus for the next 63 days to create routines that will predictably lead to the success and 'TEARS of joy' you aspire to?

2. Assuming you answered yes, then act on any or all of the following strategies.

3. Ensure your vision is clear, and your desire to make it a reality in your life is strong. Without clarity and desire, you will trip up.

4. Deal with all limiting beliefs. Refer to Chapter 5 if you need help with this.

5. Seriously assess, change if required, the people you associate with, what you read, watch, and listen to help support this journey.

6. Print off the 63-day checklist or create your own and determine the things you want to change.

7. Simply focus on winning each day, tick the box and celebrate. Then, simply repeat this process <u>every</u> day for 63 days.

8. Do it every day, even when you don't feel like it, don't think you can or don't want to.

9. Each day, focus beyond the discomfort and imagine the life you will be living when you have created the routines that will predictably lead to reality.

CHAPTER 14

Success is predictable

"Follow the process and enjoy the predictable success that follows."

I f you are reading this chapter, and if you have applied the strategies in the 'TEARS of joy' process to this point, then you have nothing more to worry about. Success is predictable. Have you ever heard the saying: *success is a journey, not a destination*? I have heard about it for many years, but haven't believed it until quite recently. For me the journey to what I wanted to achieve has been inconvenient, uncomfortable, and sometimes un-fun! So, in my mind, all I wanted to do was get to the other side of the messy and painful process to the place when I was a professional footballer, a published author, a successful business owner, and lean, fit, and healthy.

All I focused on, worried about, and doubted for a long time, was whether I was good enough and whether would I get there. I now know that my success has been the predictable result of my thoughts, emotions, actions, and routines. I didn't need to stress, worry, doubt, or be so intense all the time. Beyond any shadow of a doubt, I now know that success is a journey, not a destination. You will arrive at the destination, no need to worry, if you pay attention to the journey. That being the case, there's not much more to talk about in this book, except for you to embrace the first four steps in the 'TEARS of joy' process. In fact, just one, the first one, the thoughts you choose to focus on. This one gets the whole process in motion and heading in the direction of your dreams, purpose, and life of joyful longevity.

Seeing life as an adventure and success in each day

You will know, if you are old enough to read this, that life has challenges. In fact, you and I, as well as the whole world, has recently experienced a major challenge. Or, as I like to refer to it these days, an adventure! It's mid-2021 as I am finishing this book and getting it ready to be published, and wasn't 2020 and 2021 an adventure and a half? In fact, my 2019, 2020 and 2021 have all been wonderful adventures. If I didn't know what I know now about the power of God and that success lies in the journey, then I, like many people, would have described my last two or three years with some colourful expletives.

But interestingly, all the *adventures* I experienced have been incredible blessings in my life. That doesn't mean they have been easy or always fun, but it does mean they have all added value to my life and fuel for my purpose. This is a message I would love to help you understand and believe. What seems to be adversity is an opportunity, a problem is a gift, and a mistake is a lesson.

As I have mentioned in an earlier chapter, it was mid-2019 when my marriage ended, and it was a heartbreaking time. However, I finally began to understand my patterns and behaviours, all of which played a large part in my personal life and marital troubles. During the year I met and came to know the wonderful Dr Allan Meyer, an incredible person who is an author, speaker, pastor, mentor, and a wonderful role model for me. We each spoke at an event in June 2019, and we swapped books. I gave him a copy of my book, *The Wellness Puzzle,* and he gave me a copy of his book, *From Good Man to Valiant Man*. It is a book that has changed my life.

As I read Allan's book for the first time, it was immediately chilling. I finally understood how the male brain works and the early influences I had in my life around sexuality and women. I could finally explain behaviour and patterns that had plagued much of my adolescent and adult life. Through prayer, and the forgiveness of my sins through God's mercy and the resurrection of Christ, I finally got to the point where I was able to start forgiving myself. I started getting excited because I knew this would help me move forward in my life and my next relationship. What an incredible gift Allan Meyer and his book has been in my life.

I have said for many years, *nothing is bad, it's all content for your book!* Then COVID hit and turned the world upside down. My goodness, the years 2020 and 2021 for me can only be described in one word – adventure! The adventure of living alone, going into lockdown, and being forced to get to know and get to love myself, has been an exhilarating rollercoaster ride. After losing my speaking gigs and a large percentage of my income, the adventure of transforming my business into an online and global platform has been a wild ride. After years of talking about it, the adventure finally started with my podcast, and has been an incredible joy. The adventure of meeting, connecting, and collaborating with some incredible people has been a godsend. The adventure of watching the world changed for the better (I believe), and people start to adapt and overcome adversity has been a gift.

What I am trying to say here is that success is not always an achievement or an outcome. Success is an attitude. When you can find success in the lessons, opportunities and gifts that come out of adversity, challenges, and problems, then you will truly start to experience the adventure, joy and abundant success life has to offer.

The most important message I want to communicate in this chapter is that success is not for the lucky ones. It's not for the most talented, the most intelligent, the ones with the most money, most resources, or most contacts. Success is 100 per cent for anyone willing to think the right thoughts, manoeuvre themselves into the right emotional state, take the right actions, create the right routines, and persist with a powerful vision in their heart and mind. You can do that. It all starts with the question, what do you want?

Success is about the journey...

Ed Sheeran is one of Britain's, and the world's, biggest success stories in entertainment. I want to share a little of his story because many people look at him and think he's lucky because of his natural ability and good looks. Well, he has not achieved what he has today because of either of those things, but because he followed the 'TEARS of joy' model.

In referring to and taking quotes from www.goalcast.com, an article on this website about Ed Sheeran starts with:

> *'Ever wonder how Ed Sheeran'+s life story goes like? Well, he – like many of us – didn't have it easy. Dealing with his fair share of struggles, from bullying to inner battles, insecurity, and shame, to becoming an award-winning singer, Ed Sheeran's story shows how the artist learned to embrace his uniqueness and overcame his challenges in order to bring us one of the most beautiful voices of our time.'*

Does it sound familiar as you work towards the dreams that are driving you?

Ed Sheeran was born with some serious physical disadvantages that many would see as barriers, and use as excuses. The first was his bright orange hair. The second was, after surgery that went wrong, he was left with a lazy eye. The third was a serious speech impediment. You would think these challenges would be a barrier to a career in music and singing. For the people without a vision and passion, maybe, but not Ed.

If, as children, we had to choose the three things we would not want to have to deal with going through the challenging childhood and teen years, I think most of us would choose bright red hair, large thick glasses, and a stutter. Well, Ed had to deal with all three. While he struggled with socialising in school, he had an interest in music from a young age. He became part of a church choir at four and soon started playing the guitar. At eleven, he was already writing songs. Not only was his love for music obvious, but his commitment to developing and honing his talent started being noticed by others around him.

Ed was bullied every day at school for his stutter and oversized glasses. Whenever he tried speaking up in class, his mouth would freeze, and no words would come out. The other kids laughed at him and ridiculed him. So, understandably, he stopped participating and raising his hand at all. Surprisingly, that wasn't the case when it came to singing and playing music. He loved singing in the local church and said that playing the guitar in his room was the only time he felt in control.

His red hair clearly wasn't helping him with his cool image in school. However, he realised early on the way he looked would not determine his success. He chose to act and use his hair colour to his advantage to make something happen. In fact, by his own admission, it's what saved him as a musician:

> 'Being ginger can seem like a bad thing when you are young, but as a musician, it has been my saving grace – because if you see a ginger kid on TV and there is only one messy-haired ginger kid who plays the guitar, it is very easy to find them on YouTube.'

Speech therapy wasn't going well for Ed, his stutter wasn't improving, and one of his biggest fears was that he would be like that for the rest of his life. But things changed when one day, his dad brought him Eminem's record. He was amazed by how fast the singer was rapping. This inspired him, and he learned every word by the time he was ten. He began writing more of his own music, and suddenly, even miraculously, his stutter was gone.

Ed knew music was his calling, and he had to do something about it. So, in addition to playing the guitar and writing songs, he started performing in different venues. Soon Ed had twelve shows in a week. That continued for four years and, not long after, he was recording CDs and selling them. At the age of fourteen, Ed Sheeran took his guitar, packed some clothes, and headed to London to officially start his music career and see where it would take him.

It seems like it would have been a straight path from there, doesn't it? It was far from it. Being on the road was not easy. There were many nights he couldn't find a bed and slept in parks or in the subway. He had some nights when he didn't have any money for food and was often on the verge of giving up. But he didn't. He kept thinking about the dream he had of making it big.

In London he played in small venues, producing more of his own music, releasing albums, auditioning, and collaborating with singers he met along the way. He played in more than 300 shows in 2009 alone, but he just didn't seem to be getting closer to his big break. It finally came in 2010. While it wouldn't have been possible without the hard work and everything Ed had done, social media helped his success happen faster. Not many singers were leveraging the potential of social media channels at the time. However Ed quickly spotted its potential and finally saw the value of his ginger hair! He was posting his videos online, and one of them was noticed by the rapper Example, who liked his style so much that he invited him to tour with his band. The rest, as they say in the classics, is history.

I think we would agree that while Ed did have some talent and aptitude for music, that's not the main reason for his global astronomical success as an entertainer. I think we could agree while social media and YouTube helped him get his face and music out to the world, it was only a small part of the picture. You may even say he was lucky he had bright ginger hair because it helped him stand out as an entertainer. I think it would be fair to say he has achieved his status to this point in his life by following the 'TEARS of joy' model.

He started thinking and visualising at a young age that music was something he wanted to pursue. Irrespective of his challenges, it helped him feel positive, excited, and determined. This led him to the action he took, singing in the church choir at the age of four, learning to play the guitar, writing songs at eleven, and learning rap songs. These actions became powerful and unconscious routines for Ed. As he improved, his vision for what he wanted became clearer and clearer. With his clear vision, positive thoughts, and strong desire, he overcame all obstacles in his life to fulfil his wonderful vision. Ed Sheeran is no more special than you are or I am, he just followed a predictable path, and the results he got were not a surprise.

Colonel Harland Sanders is a legend in my mind, and certainly not because of the food KFC produces, but because of his courage and commitment to creating 'TEARS of joy' in his life. He was not lucky, talented, rich, or connected when he started on his journey. In fact, if anything, he would have most likely been considered as unlucky, untalented, broke, and alone. So how does someone with no money, no friends, no home, and no real talent make it so big, and for so long beyond his death? Simple, it's the predictable SUCCESS that comes after the TEAR!

As a broke pensioner with nowhere to live and not much going for him, all Harland Sanders had was a thought. That thought was about the great recipe for southern fried chicken he had, and how much people had enjoyed it over the years. He started thinking about what he could do with that recipe and, because he was open to ideas, one dropped into his head. His idea was to approach fast food outlets, give them his recipe to make amazing southern fried chicken, and ask them to simply pay him a percentage of the chicken sales. It sounded like a good idea to Harland, and it got him excited.

With a clear vision for a better life, as I described earlier in the book, a burning desire to make it happen and strong positive emotion about the thought he had generated, he went into action. Now, just to remind you in case you forget, his first action and approach to a restaurant was unsuccessful. He stayed focused on his dream, and he approached the next restaurant. Again, unsuccessful. Feeling a little discouraged, he got up and went again. Yes, you guessed it, the same result. He acted every day, irrespective of the fact that he was getting no after no. He got to 63 days and, while he experienced no luck, he had created a strong routine that would carry him to astronomical success. It was fortuitous that he stuck at it for those 63 days because he ended up getting 1009 rejections before he received his first yes. Do you think there may have been some 'TEARS of joy' when this happened? I think so!

I enjoy talking about well-known people, and I am inspired by the stories that led to their wonderful success. For every famous actor, athlete, businessperson, musician, explorer, inventor, politician, entre-preneur, philanthropist, or other celebrity, there are hundreds of people who quietly go about their daily lives, achieving incredible things, and 'TEARS of joy', without any hype or fanfare. I am blessed to be the child of two of those people.

I have referred many times to my mother, who passed away in 2004. Since my book about her was published, I have spoken to many thousands of people about her inspiring journey with cancer, and the fact that she outlived the medical prediction for her life by fifteen years. She truly experienced 'TEARS of joy' in those years, and I am grateful that I was there for many of those joyful moments.

The other person in my life who has always been an incredible rock and blessing is my father, Bill. Much like my mother, he was never after fanfare or recognition. He just did what he had to do to be a great husband and father who supported, loved, and protected his family. He did, and still does do, an amazing job. At 86 years old, as I write this, he is still the man I respect, love, and look up to most in the whole world.

My father was an only child born to a beautiful couple who, like many young couples, had no idea how to show affection to their young son. In fact, so ill-equipped were they to be parents, they very quickly bundled him up and sent him off to a boarding school in Geelong, two hours from where they lived in Melbourne, Australia. My dad had to learn to survive the hard way, growing up in a tough all-male boarding school environment in the 1940s and '50s. Once he had mastered survival, he quickly developed an interest in geology, and followed that passion through his secondary and tertiary education and came out the other end as a qualified geologist.

Like many of us as teenagers, we never really think through career choices. My father discovered his career as a geologist was remarkably interesting for him. However, it would not give him the time, money, or options he wanted in his life or for his family. So what would he do? He really had no other skills or qualifications, and he was – and still is – a very shy person who prefers to keep to himself. He tried his hand working in a business owned by my mother's parents, but that was not the answer. Then in the 1970s, he had a thought.

I now know where my propensity for illogical thinking comes from. My father is not spontaneous like I am and, in fact, is the total opposite. On this occasion, however, he followed through on what would seem to be an irrational but nevertheless extremely exciting thought. He identified a massive gap in the marketplace, and saw an opportunity. Computers were just becoming more common in workplaces, and there was a lack of people who could manage, repair, and build systems. So my father, with a geological background, launched off and taught himself computer systems and became a computer systems analyst.

How did he do that, based on his total lack of skills, qualifications, and experience in that space? Why did he do it, specially considering the early stage of computers in Australia and the world? I mean, let's face it. In the 1970s, a microchip was a crumb left in the packet of potato chips, a gigabyte was getting supersized at McDonald's, a laptop was a small pet, and a USB came from outer space! He did it because of a thought. The thought was that he wanted to create a better life for his family, and he saw an opportunity in the computing space. That's all he needed to know at the time.

The thought empowered and excited him, and those feelings moved him into action. He is truly a detail-oriented man, so he studied, learned, and acted until his routine led him to amazing success. He truly was ahead of his time and was one of the very few people who could do what he did at that stage of history in Australia. He became in demand and was very highly paid. He took his money, invested, and set up self-managed superannuation funds. With work, focus, persistence, and the right routines, he predictably created financial independence at an early age.

When my mother was diagnosed with secondary liver cancer, they decided to make her life and recovery a priority. My dad was able to retire from work and be always on the journey with his wife. As I write this, that was over thirty years ago. For fifteen years, the things they did together bought many 'TEARS of joy' for them and all of us as a family.

I genuinely want you to discard the thought that you are not good enough to create any success you can visualise and desire. I want you to let go of logic, release common sense, and grasp tightly to hope and faith. You see, all success in life starts out as a crazy, unreasonable, irrational, and illogical idea. Again, keep your mind fixed on the descriptions of faith by author Phillip Yancey. He said: '*faith means trusting in advance what will only make sense in reverse*'. Also, the one from the Bible, Hebrews 11:1 – '*Faith is the substance of things hoped for, the evidence of things not seen*'. In other words, with the right thoughts and empowering emotions which initiate an action, it can develop a powerful routine. Predictable success will be the outcome, no matter how unlikely it may seem from the outset.

Throughout history, even the most famous and successful people had to deal with criticism and the opinions of knowledgeable and influential people who believed they weren't good enough. Yet, they were able to create 'TEARS of joy' because, no matter how unlikely success may have seemed, they followed the process. Here are a few of them (from www. vironika.org):

- The Beatles were rejected by record label after record label. One notable response was '*guitar groups are on the way out*' and '*the Beatles have no future in show business*'.
- In her search to be published, one of the forty-plus rejection letters JK Rowling received claimed: '*Children just aren't interested in witches and wizards anymore*'.
- Winston Churchill's father said that Winston was '*unfit for a career in law or politics*'.
- Barbara Streisand's mother said she'd never be a singer because her voice wasn't good enough, and she'd never be pretty enough to be an actor.
- Henry Morton, the Stevens Institute of Technology president, commented about Thomas Edison's light bulb: '*Everyone acquainted with the subject will recognize it as a conspicuous failure*'.

- A modelling agency told Marilyn Monroe: *'You better get secretarial work or get married'*.
- In a famous rejection letter, Rudyard Kipling was told by the San Francisco Examiner: *'I'm sorry, Mr Kipling, but you just don't know how to use the English language'*.
- Henry Ford was told that *'the horse is here to stay, but the automobile is only a novelty, a fad'*.

An article in www.theguardian.com about **Oprah Winfrey** starts with:

> *'Oprah Winfrey was four-and-a-half years old, when she decided she wasn't going to have the life expected of her. She was raised on a small Mississippi farm by her grandmother, whose highest hope for her granddaughter was that when she became someone's domestic worker, she would be treated kindly by her employers. "I just hope you get some good white folks when you grow up, treat you right, treat you nice," Winfrey said her grandmother told her.'*

We all know that Oprah Winfrey did a little better than getting a good job as someone's domestic worker. How does someone, coming from such a poor and underprivileged childhood, create such abundant success and make such a profound impact on the world? Well certainly not luck, that's for sure. It was the predictable result of the 'TEARS of joy' process that started with the thought that *she wasn't going to have the life expected of her*.

Have you ever heard of a singer named **Elvis Presley**? Who hasn't? Even since he died in 1977 at the young age of 42, the impact he left on the music world has grown and still grows stronger every day. He is the most famous singer in history, yet time after time, Elvis was told that he couldn't sing. At the age of fourteen, he achieved a C-grade for music, *below average*, with his teacher specifically commenting that he *'had no aptitude for singing'*.

Later in life, Elvis auditioned for a local quartet. He was not success-ful, again because of his perceived lack of talent. After a performance at Nashville's *Grand Ole Opry*, the concert hall manager told Elvis he was better off being a truck driver as he would never make it as a singer. Elvis didn't quit because his vision was strong, his thoughts fixed, and his desire unstoppable. Instead, he studied gospel and blues records until Sun Records producer Sam Phillips discovered him. So, again I ask, how did Elvis become a global phenomenon, with such regular and damning criticism about his ability? I don't need to tell you, do I?

I could go on and on here, but I won't because I'm pretty sure you've got the message. That message is simple. All this success has little to do with a person's talent, education, intellect, or the other things you may be using as your excuse not to try. Get a clear and strong vision of what you want, think about its success, move the positive and powerful emo-tions into action, and keep going until your unconscious routines will predictably lead you to the success you are after.

Moving towards 'TEARS of Joy'

> Philippians 4:13 – *I can do all things through him who strengthens me.* (ESV)

There's not a lot more I need to add in this chapter. It is my greatest hope and desire that, as you have been reading this book, you have been implementing the suggestions and strategies along the way. If so, you may already be experiencing some of the success I have discussed in this chapter. If you've just been reading and wondering if this could work for you, trust me when I say it can, and it will, on the condition you are willing to do the work suggested in this book. All I want to do right now is encourage you to take a leap of faith and give it a go. You've got nothing to lose, just your best life, and 'TEARS of joy' to gain.

The key, and certainly what I've found in my life, is to get a clear picture in your head of what you want, then very quickly move it from your head into your heart. This is what will get the 'TEARS of joy' journey into motion. Think big, think less, feel more, and action will be the result. An incredible life is there for you, no matter what stage you are at, or what you have experienced in your past. Follow the process and enjoy the predictable success that follows.

Key questions and action steps

1. It is time to be honest with yourself because this is only a book, and it can't change your life. You must do that. Are you ready?
2. Do you have a clear vision of what success looks like for yourself? If not, please spend some time to get the picture and clarity about why it's important in your life.
3. The main key to the success I've spoken about in this chapter is a strong desire. Do you have it for what you want?
4. If you've answered yes to the previous question, then simply get started with the 'TEARS of joy' process, as the hardest of the work is done.
5. I've shared lots of evidence and anecdotes from many people who have created incredible success in their lives. This is not because of talent but because of the predictable outcome of following through on this process. Do you believe you can do the same?
6. If you answered yes, get started. If you answered no, you need to believe that you are GOOD ENOUGH, which you are!
7. Now stop worrying, stop doubting, and start acting. The success you want will be the predictable result of the routines you develop because of your actions from the emotions you experience due to the thoughts you choose to focus on.

CHAPTER 15

The butterfly effect

"Now is your time to focus on and achieve your own 'TEARS of joy' and, in the process, you will help many other people do the same."

In case you didn't know, you are part of something much bigger than yourself. You are part of a family, a community, a city, a country, and a world. Do you believe the impact of the thoughts you have, the emotions you experience and the choices you make can ripple out and impact people's lives on the other side of the world? Well, I will tell you without fear of contradiction, you <u>will</u> have that kind of powerful impact, whether you know about it, or believe it. It's called the butterfly effect. The following paragraph is taken from *Wikipedia* at the time of this writing:

> *The term is closely associated with the work of mathematician and meteorologist Edward Lorenz. He noted that the butterfly effect is derived from the metaphorical example of the details of a tornado (the exact time of formation, the exact path taken) being influenced by minor perturbations such as a distant butterfly flapping its wings several weeks*

earlier. Lorenz discovered the effect when he observed runs of his weather model with initial condition data that were rounded in a seemingly inconsequential manner. He noted that the weather model would fail to reproduce the results of runs with the unrounded initial condition data. A very small change in initial conditions had created a signifi-cantly different outcome.'

Now, can a butterfly, just by the flapping of its wings, cause enough movement of air molecules to cause a tornado on the other side of the world? I don't know. What I do know is that the things you think, say, and do, which may seem insignificant, will have a profound ripple effect on your life and the lives of many other people for many years, even generations. I recently listened to an inspiring audio titled *The Butterfly Effect* and want to share an amazing series of true stories that seem separate but are connected by the power of the butterfly or ripple effect.

In 1970, a Norwegian-American man named Dr Norman Borlaug (1914-2009) won the *Nobel Peace Prize* for a lifetime of work to feed a hungry world. Dr Borlaug developed successive generations of wheat varieties with broad and stable disease resistance, broad adaptation to growing conditions across many degrees of latitude, and exceedingly high yield potential. As a result of his work, he was able to save millions of lives. So it seems like he was deserving of that prize and honour. Unless that is, you want to give it to Henry A Wallace.

Henry A Wallace (1888-1965) was the 11th USA Secretary of Agriculture and 33rd Vice President of the USA to President Roosevelt, with a background and passion for farming and agriculture. Henry Wallace suggested that President Roosevelt employ someone to develop wheat crops that could survive in all weather conditions. Roosevelt agreed and gave Wallace the responsibility of finding the right per-son. After much research and many interviews, Henry Wallace decided upon a relatively unknown person for the job. He appointed Dr Norman Borlaug. So, maybe Henry Wallace should have been given the *Nobel Peace Prize*. Unless that is, you want to give it to George Washington-Carver.

George Washington-Carver (1860-1943) had a tough childhood, born into slavery in Diamond, Missouri. After his parents passed away, he was encouraged to develop an interest in plants and soon became a brilliant biology student. He even took graduate work and, upon graduation, was offered a teaching position at Iowa State University. He was the first black teacher that Iowa State had ever hired. While there, Washington-Carver used to take long walks in the surrounding fields to study plants for research. On some of these walks, he took a little friend with him, the six-year-old son of a science professor. Washington-Carver shared his love of plants, and the boy responded enthusiastically. At the age of eleven, that boy began doing experiments with different varieties of corn. His name was Henry A Wallace.

It was this encouragement from George Washington-Carver that excited Henry A Wallace to develop his interest in farming. When he became Vice President of the USA, it inspired him to employ someone to develop wheat crops that could survive in all weather conditions, which led to Norman Borlaug being appointed and then winning the *Nobel Peace Prize*. So, should George Washington-Carver have received the prize? Maybe, unless you think Moses Carver is more deserving.

Moses Carver (1812-1910) was a wealthy man who owned land, employed, and housed a young couple. The lady of the couple had just given birth weeks before her husband was killed, and she with her new baby boy were kidnapped by night raiders from Arkansas. It was the middle of winter and freezing cold, but Moses jumped on his horse to track them down and save them. When he finally found the raiders, he negotiated a trade. The mother had been killed, but the raiders threw a toe-sack across the creek, and, as it thudded to the ground, Moses heard a groan. Inside was the baby boy, starving and suffering from exposure to the cold weather.

The raiders had taken Moses' horse and all his valuables, so he took the baby boy and wrapped him in a warm blanket. He walked back home, which took days, holding the baby close to his body to keep him warm. All the way, he spoke to the baby: "You are safe now. Your mother is gone, your father is gone, but I will be your new father and raise you as my own." Moses Carver had just adopted the son of Mary Washington and named him George. George went on to study and teach biology, influence a boy named Henry A Wallace, who became the Vice President of the USA. He then appointed Norman Borlaug, who developed wheat varieties that won him the *Nobel Peace Prize*. So, why not give it to Moses Carver?

Moses Carver was born in 1812, and Norman Borlaug won the *Nobel Peace Prize* in 1970. Would he have won the award if Moses Carver didn't become wealthy and employ Mary Washington and her husband? No, he would not. Do you know what that is? That's the butterfly effect, the most powerful and life-transforming phenomenon on the planet.

Your thoughts are things. They lead to words, attitudes and actions that will ripple and impact many lives for generations to come. Your words, attitudes and actions will impact others, just as the words, attitudes and actions of others have impacted you. In the book, *The Happiness Advantage,* the author Shawn Achor refers to another book called *Connected*. In this book, the co-authors Nicholas Christakis and James Fowler draw on years of research to show how our words, attitudes, and actions constantly cascade and bounce off each other in every way and direction.

Their theory is that words, attitudes, and actions don't just impact and infect the people we interact with directly, like our family, friends, and colleagues. Their research suggests that each individual influence appears to extend to people within three degrees. So, when you choose and make positive change in your own life, you have unconsciously influenced the words, attitudes, and actions of an incredible number of people.

James Fowler explains in his life: *'I know that I am not just having an impact on my son, I'm potentially having an impact on my son's best friend's mother'*. This influence ripples out and adds up. Fowler and Christakis estimate that there are approximately 1,000 people within three degrees of most of us. Some less and some much more. This is powerful stuff. This is simply a result of you and me trying to be the best we can, and create our own 'TEARS of joy'. We are unknowingly yet positively impacting and improving the lives of 1,000 people, or many more, around the world. But what about the people within three degrees of those 1,000 people? Are you getting my drift here?

My mother passed away in 2004, yet the impact of her life is still being felt by many people. It will continue to positively influence people for infinite generations to come. Let me tell you, her courage and inspiration have extended way beyond three degrees of her. How? Well, the thing you need to know about my amazing mother is how humble she was. Just three months before she passed, I remember sitting down with her and telling her that I would write a book about her life, her journey with cancer, and her inspiration. She looked at me with a quizzical look on her face. She genuinely asked: "Andrew, honestly, who would be interested in me and my story?"

Well, my beautiful mother, the answer to that question is hard to put into an actual number, but it is much more than 1,000, that's for sure. She fought a disease that never relented for fifteen years longer than was predicted. She made changes in her life that didn't just give her more time but also transformed her life experience. She is an inspiring example of the quote that says: *'Life is not measured by the numbers of breaths we take but by the moments that take our breath away'*. I can tell you that her immediate family, close friends, and associates were inspired and impacted by her courage, determination, and willingness to change. I can also tell you that many tens of thousands of people, maybe hundreds of thousands of people, maybe even millions of people, will be impacted by this simple, humble lady.

The book I wrote about her, *Dance Until It Rains,* was published in 2011. It's now 2021. As I write this book ten years later, I know *Dance Until It Rains* has traversed the world, and her message is impacting and inspiring people every day. In just 2019 and 2020 alone, I estimate I spoke to 200-250 audiences, conservatively averaging fifty people in each audience. If you do the maths, that's 10,000 to 12,500 people. I talk about creating a purposeful life of joyful longevity. I always talk about my mother, her courage and her inspiring journey and intend to keep doing it for many more years to come. Can you even begin to imagine the number of lives directly or indirectly impacted by her legacy, and then incredibly, those within three degrees of all those people? It's mind-blowing and incomprehensible, to say the least.

My mother was a scared little Hungarian girl who came from her homeland on a boat for six months, at four years of age, to settle in a country she'd never heard of. She had to come to terms with a language she couldn't speak. She was not famous but has impacted and will continue to impact millions of lives for many generations to come. That's the ripple effect, a power we all have. Yes, even you! It's easy to look at people like Nelson Mandela, Mother Teresa, Oprah Winfrey, Steve Jobs, Richard Branson, JK Rowling, Fred Hollows, and many other well-known people who have impacted lives. But what about you? You are impacting lives right now. As you go about your day, and be the best you can be, you influence people's thoughts, emotions, actions, routines, and consequent success in life, not to mention the people they will impact. What you do today will ripple out and be felt across many miles and many generations by many people. Do you believe that?

Let me now tell you a story behind the story of my mother. As you know, she came to Australia from Hungary on a boat at the tender and fearful age of four years. It was a terrifying time for a young girl. Her parents were stressed, anxious, distracted, and unable to comfort her the way she needed to feel loved. From a young age, she started to believe that she was not unconditionally loved by her parents but had to work hard to earn any love she received.

My mother, in desperate need of the wonderful feeling of unconditional love, received a letter from her grandmother on her sixth birthday. Now, this letter, as you will work out very quickly, was written by someone who had a very limited grasp of the English language. What you will also get from it – in fact, it pours off the page – is the total, heartfelt and unconditional love from a grandmother to her granddaughter.

```
My dear, sweet, little Susy. I will wright to You, in Fnglish for ᴛ want you
shall understand every word of my letter,ᴛ hope it will arrive intime, to Your
birhday.I send vou my angel,thousand, and thousen kisses, and I am so sorry
not to bee by You and not kiss You with the greatest love on this day. Now
You are 6,year old, an adult young girl, who is going to scool, and learning
and tehaving himself surely very good, and who also helping,at his parents, in
the shop, and also in the household.But ᴛ hope you d,ont forget, to play much
with your little frindes, you send in a letter some nice wordss to us,that
You are learning about the good god in school.Please pray to Him every evening
before going sleeping, that he shall hdp us,to come aut to You, and than I w
newer will be sorry,and we would learn together, but also play, and take walk
and swimming in the sea , would,nt it bee wonderfull? It will come to you a
hungarian young man, who will bring you a little bralet of gold, with a heart,
and another joujou, it is the birthday present of the two grandmother,gyönr
gyösi and lellei. Wear it,in health, and shall brin you fortune my dear.
Next You must personelly, describe me, what did you got for x.mas, and how di
did You celebrated, the birthday, of your Daddy, and yours, and bp did cooked
Your mammy, and how do you like uncle Andrew, an your aunty Flisabeth.
                    I embrace, you with the greatest love.so many time, that
You will be unable to cont it.
                    Your
                            lellei nagymama.  Margaret Fabinyi
Bpest. 1941.jan.11.
```

This letter, as you can see, was written in January 1941. My mother passed away in December 2004. She had this letter with her that whole time. That's 63 years! The paper is old, frayed, tear-stained, and has been folded and unfolded many times. However, that message of unconditional love is strong. It helped my mother through many challenging times in childhood, youth, adulthood, motherhood, and as she dealt with cancer. It was one of the reasons, I believe, she fought so hard for so long. It was the ripple effect of a grandmother's deep and unconditional love she had in her heart to share with her own family for as long as humanly possible. That ripple effect reached my mother, who passed it on and continued the wave impacting many people during her lifetime, and in the many years since she left this Earth.

Even today, I am continually using this letter as an example of the power of the ripple effect of the written word. Do you honestly think that my great grandmother, as she sat down to type that letter in January 1941, would have believed its impact? Do you think she would have even considered that her great grandson would be using it, 80 years later, in his speaking, his writing, and his life, to help inspire other people? Who knows how much longer the butterfly effect of this letter will continue? The thought about its phenomenal and ongoing impact excites me every day.

I love how God works. The things happening in my life right now are powerfully reinforcing this message of the butterfly effect. For a while, I have been talking about being on a mission to create a wave of wellness around the world. I am passionate and purpose-driven to help people live a life of joyful longevity. In fact, I have just recently finished up a multi session 63-day *Joyful Longevity* program with an organisation. As I delivered the last wrap up session, it was mind-blowing to me in terms of the ripple effect of small, seemingly insignificant actions.

The people who chose to participate in this program had to do just a few very simple things. The first was to identify what was most important in their life and keep them on track for 63-days to create a strong embedded behaviour change. The next thing they had to do was choose a small number of very basic actions they wanted to develop into powerful routines. Thirdly, they had to simply act, tick the box, and win every day for 63-days. They were supported and encouraged throughout this process.

As I sat down with them at the final session, I asked them to share their experiences. What I heard was incredibly inspiring and gratifying to me. These people, in just 63-days, had changed their own lives and, without even realising it, impacted people around them. One lady shared how the one and only action she committed to was to eat a healthy breakfast every day for 63 days. As you can see, it's a simple choice and one that you wouldn't necessarily believe could make much of a difference. Well, I stood there listening to this lady, stunned at what she said.

She started talking about some of the personal benefits she had experienced. When she mentioned she had more energy, I wasn't surprised. When she discussed how it helped her with her moods and food choices during the day, I was pretty much expecting that. When she explained that the way she was feeling had inspired her to drink more water and start doing more walking, I was gaining interest. When she declared she had dropped two dress sizes, I was amazed. Then, the next thing she discussed brought tears (of joy) to my eyes.

She had started getting up earlier, preparing her breakfast and taking the time to eat it. A few days after she had been doing it regularly, her son started joining her. As she was talking about this, you could see her getting emotional. She explained how her son would normally just rush out the door, say very little to her, with no breakfast or with something unhealthy. Now, every morning, he sits with her, eating a healthy breakfast and connecting with his mother. Then, when her husband saw what was happening, he joined them as well. Wow! Can you see how that one tiny, seemingly insignificant decision to eat breakfast that she stuck to for 63 days had rippled and had a massive influence on herself, her son, her husband, her relationships and... who else?

In the same room, on the same day, was the man who explained that just a couple of months earlier, he was angry, unhealthy, and recently diagnosed with a condition for which there was supposedly no cure. He decided to make some simple changes, be happy, stop drinking alcohol, and eat breakfast. The first butterfly effect miracle from these decisions occurred when he went back to his doctor for a check-up, just a few days before sharing this with the group. At that appointment, his doctor's jaw hit the floor when, after the tests had been done, he found that the condition was completely gone from his patient's body! Now, I don't know what the reason was for the miracle cure. It could have been God's grace. It may have been the changes he made on the program, as I can't imagine they didn't help. Whatever the reason, the butterfly effect really began due to the impact this had, is having, and will continue to have on his family and the people they influence. His change in moods initially confused his family, but then started to bring them all closer together.

The last quick story I want to share from this same meeting is about the man who had identified himself as a workaholic, and wanted to focus his 63-days on getting home earlier and reconnecting with his family. He admitted it was a struggle because he had a deeply entrenched belief that he needed to be at work and had a strong habit of overworking. He felt responsible for being at the beck-and-call of work when he was needed. He focused over the 63-days, and wasn't sure that it had the impact he wanted until the last day, day number 63! It was a Sunday, and he was out working in the garden. His son, who never enjoyed gardening, came out and spent the afternoon with his dad, helping him and connecting with him. Again, as this man described this, you could see his emotion and just how important it was for him.

The power of the butterfly effect was at work. It has only just begun in these people's lives because their new thoughts, words, and actions will continue to ripple out three degrees, and then for many years and generations to come.

Moving towards 'TEARS of Joy'

> Matthew 5:16 – *In the same way, let your light shine before others, that they may see your good deeds and glorify your Father in heaven.* (NIV)

You are an amazing miracle. Did you know, and do you believe that? Were you aware that the chances you are even born, and on this planet, are so infinitesimally small that it would be impossible to calculate? Let's just start with the chances of your parents being born and then randomly meeting, building a relationship, and then taking it to the next level. Then in that wonderful moment of conception, the chances of you being created were around 300 million to one. That's about how many sperm rush vigorously in pursuit of fertilising that one solitary egg. You were that sperm who overcame and beat all the others in the race to get to the ovum and push your way in. Can you see that, before you were even born, you had courage, resilience, persistence, and were an absolute winner?

So, if we worked backwards from that moment of your conception and you tried to calculate the odds of your existence, your head would probably explode! From the 300 million sperm you had to beat, the chances of your parents' meeting, the 300 million to one chance that each of them was born, the chances of both sets of your grandparent's meeting, being born, then your great grandparents, great great grandparents, and so on, all the way back through the generations. Are you getting my drift? Now, that's what I call an incredible butterfly effect!

Do you really think, with such minuscule odds, that you being alive and reading this book is luck? Do you truly believe it was a random event, or that you were a mistake? I don't think so. Your life on this planet was planned, pre-ordained, meant-to-be, and you are here for a purpose. All the things that had to happen, and fall into place to bring you here, result from the powerful ripple effect that makes life and achievement on this planet seem like it is magic. It's not magic, but you are a miracle.

So, what does that mean for you, your life, and the lives of people you influence? It means you have a responsibility. We all have that same responsibility to be the best we can be, find our true purpose, live honestly, courageously, and authentically to our own value system, and influence and inspire others to do the same. You will inspire others, whether you think you will or not. You will impact lives within three degrees of you, whether you want to or not. You will impact the generations and leave a legacy, whether you believe it or not.

Now is your time to focus on and achieve your own 'TEARS of joy' and, in the process, you will help many generations of other people do the same.

Key questions and action steps

1. How has your life been impacted by the influence of another person? Has that same person impacted other lives? Why? What did they do or say?
2. Who have you influenced through your own beliefs, thoughts, words, and actions?
3. Can you see how your influence on even just one person will ripple out and impact others?
4. What are the types of habits you would like the people close to you to adopt? Are they the ones you currently have?
5. This is the time to reflect and assess your own beliefs, thoughts, words, and actions and see how they could possibly start the butterfly effect that will impact other lives.

6. If you truly believed this was the case, and that your beliefs, thoughts, words, and actions would impact other people, would you keep doing what you are doing?
7. Make a list of the things you would change.
8. Start today to implement these changes.

CHAPTER 16

The plan: start today

"Your life is short. You only get one go at it. Make it your best. Fill it with 'TEARS of joy' experiences and live a truly wonderful life of joyful longevity."

As an author, one of my goals is that you will be reading this last chapter. So, as you read this, just know I have a warm feeling in my heart as it means I have held your attention right till the end, and that pleases me, so thank you for being here. There is no doubt I am a determined change-maker, and every time I write a book or speak to a group, my mission is to deliver as passionately as I can. However, if my message entertains and interests you but doesn't lead you to action, I have failed. Honestly, as much as I enjoy writing, I am not a fiction writer – as you can clearly tell – I am a writer of self-empowerment material. As much as I want to inform, engage, and inspire you, my mission is to empower you to action. If you put the book down after finishing it and say to yourself it was a good book, but do nothing different, then neither I nor the book has done the intended job.

Having said that, I want to ask you this. Are you wanting to change, ready for change and willing to start? There needs to be a trigger point, doesn't there? A need, a want, a desire, an *aha moment*, a *light-bulb moment*, a *turning point*, or whatever you want to call it. That's the moment when it goes from a nice idea to something that is non-negotiable and must be done. My greatest desire is for you to get to that point before a crisis in your life requires action, and you do it now while you have the choice. So, let me ask you a few questions that, if you answer honestly, may help move you closer to that point. It may even push you over the edge to action – if you haven't already started, that is.

> **Question One** – Suppose you keep doing what you are doing in certain areas of your life. Will it enhance or erode your ability to enjoy what's most important to you?

> **Question Two** – Who is watching you, and whose lives are you influencing that you may not even realise? Do you want them to have similar habits and outcomes in life to you?

> **Question Three** – Can you identify some small things you should and could change?

> **Question Four** – What will be the benefit if you do, <u>and</u> what will be the consequence if you don't?

> **Question Five** – Are you willing and ready to make some simple changes to transform your life experience?

Well, I don't know about you, but I've just re-read those questions, and they have agitated me enough to want to make some changes in my life. What about you? If you are agitated, aggravated, motivated, stimulated, or any other 'ated' words you can think of, now is the time to act.

Don't assess it, analyse it, or over-think it. Act on it. Move it from your head to your heart and get going. Are you there? If you are, I want to give you some ideas of what to do right now. Again, that is if you haven't already started on this wonderful journey to 'TEARS of joy'.

Everything I'm going to talk about now is just a summary of what I've discussed in detail throughout this book. So, all you need to do is go back to the relevant chapter if you need more information, or I welcome you to contact me at andrew@andrewjobling.com.au if you need extra help. With any journey that you want to go on, and this is a fun and adventurous journey, you need to begin with the end in mind. I've used the analogy before about going out in your car without knowing where you are heading. If you were ever crazy enough to do that, where do you think you would end up? Either lost or back at the beginning, right? You must have a clear destination, and a strong desire to reach it, before starting on any journey. I will go to the supermarket today to get some groceries, why? I know exactly where it is, I know how to get there, and I have a strong desire to buy food to eat and live! Simple, right?

So are you ready to do this, or continue doing this? It is my desire, and even my responsibility, to help you get through at least one 63-day cycle. Once you've done it, you will understand the power of small changes and how they will ripple out and move you towards the 'TEARS of joy' you want in your life. So, let's start with this vision of what your life will look like when 'TEARS of joy' are a common occurrence.

Vision/purpose/ideal day

At this point, I will refer you back to Chapters 4 and 5 and suggest you re-read them to help you get really clear on what is most important in your life. Finding your purpose, identifying the reason you are here (when I say *here*, I mean alive and, on this planet), and focusing on what excites you, is the key to any success in life. Please don't go any further

until you have spent some time developing your vision and have some clarity on what will move you to keep moving, specially when the old thinking and pre-existing habits try to pull you back.

What is most important in your life? What, or who, would you do anything for at any time, no matter the discomfort or inconvenience? If you were to listen to your inner voice, intuition, or gut, which direction would it move you? What does that ideal day look like for you? I'm talking about a day when you have all the time, money, choices, wellbeing, and people you care about that you want and need? The sheet you can see below can be downloaded from my website at https://andrewjobling.com.au/resources-downloads/ if you would like to use it.

What is your why?

What is most important for you?

We only tend to do what will help us achieve things that are most important. What are they for you?

100 Dreams

The next part of the vision building process I want to encourage you to do is an activity that I was motivated to do some years ago. It was to write a list of 100 things I wanted to do, have, or become. It seems like a daunting task but, trust me on this, it's a game-changer. It takes ideas and theories and puts them clearly and specifically onto paper, and then, they magically become real. It will absolutely help in the foundation stage of the process. Now, 100 sounds like a lot, and I'm sure you are thinking, as I did, that you don't have 100 dreams. Trust me, you do, as did I.

I've mentioned speaker and trainer Keith Abraham before in this book. He has a wonderful free resource on his website, a *100 lifetime goals worksheet* that asks 25 questions to help you create your list of 100 lifetime dreams and goals. For these questions, go to https://keithabraham.com/free-resources/. Once you have made this list of 100 dreams and goals, you will feel empowered, excited, and unstoppable.

'TEARS of joy' worksheet

The big picture, the dream, the vision or whatever you want to call it, is the non-negotiable first step. Please don't think you can go any further into this journey without it. So, if you haven't spent time there, stop, turn around and go back to it. I want you to be successful and experience 'TEARS of joy', not *tears of frustration*. The main reason people are lost and frustrated is simple. They have NO dream, NO vision and/or NO purpose.

Once the critical foundation stage is laid, we can get more specific. To help with this next process, I want to offer the 'TEARS of joy' worksheet that I referred to earlier in the book:

Creating TEARS of Joy

SUCCESS

_____
_____
_____

ROUTINE

_____
_____
_____

_____
_____
_____

EMOTION

_____
_____
_____

THOUGHT

_____
_____
_____

Again, this resource can be downloaded from my website at https://andrewjobling.com.au/resources-downloads/. This worksheet will be a life-changing sheet of paper if you treat it like it's the most valuable thing you own. Now, here's how to create 'TEARS of joy' working backwards through the model.

Success – What is one thing, in any area of your life (that will obviously contribute to your vision, purpose and ideal day), that would represent success for you? This is a goal, and it can be a short-term goal or a long-term goal. However, try not to push the goal beyond twelve months. If you remember, the year eight boy I spoke about wanted to get a B in Science. What is your goal? Write it in the space provided on the worksheet, and write it in the following form:

> *It is [date of achievement], and I feel [describe the emotions you will experience when the goal is achieved] as I have [state the goal]. I have rewarded myself with [state the reward].*

Here's my example.

> *It is 15 September 2021. I feel excited, proud, and on purpose as I hold my eighth published book, 'TEARS of joy', in my hands. I have rewarded myself with a celebratory meal out with important people in my life.*

Routine – We all know that goals don't just accidentally, or luckily come to fruition. They don't just magically appear in your life. They take work, focus, inconvenience, persistence, lessons and, sometimes, discomfort. Again, I want to reinforce that everything you experience in your life, good or bad, is the product of the unconscious routines you develop. Positive or negative routines will create predictable results, so please don't be surprised with your success or lack of it. Just look at the routines in your life, and the answers will always be found there.

So, think about the goal you wrote in the *Success* section of the worksheet. What is a routine you will need to develop to predictably attain that result? There may be more than one. What are they? Based on my example above, the routine is simple. I need to write, edit and/or polish my manuscript <u>every day</u> until it's ready to be submitted to my publisher. What is your routine? Write it in the appropriate section of the worksheet.

Action – There is no habit or routine on the planet that didn't start with a solitary action. An action that must happen today – yes, today, not tomorrow, next week, or when you feel like it! Why? I don't know the percentages, but most people who don't immediately act on that impulse will never even take the first step. Remember, you need to move it from your head to your heart as quickly as possible, then action will happen. The longer you stay in the quicksand inside your head, the longer you will be stuck there and unable to break free. So, please take this action step today, before you go to bed tonight.

What is your action? I have done mine. You are reading it! Sometimes that initial action can be hard to decide on. If you know your action, write it on your sheet and commit to it before this day ends. If you are unsure, like my year eight friend who was about to get started on the adventure of achieving his B in Science, then I would find someone today you can get some advice from. There is no point in acting if it's not going to lead you towards the success and 'TEARS of joy' you want. I recommended the year eight boy talk to his science teacher. If you are unsure, make your action to speak to your coach, mentor, trusted friend, or someone who has done or is doing what you want. Do it today.

Emotion – As we know, it's the emotion that moves us all. Now is the time to get this idea, goal, and vision out of your head and into your heart. It needs to be a strong enough emotion to break through and overcome inertia to get you into action. I can tell you when I think about this book being finished, published, and in your hands, I get excited and determined beyond belief. Even thinking about it now has motivated me to write more today than I would normally write.

Right now, close your eyes. Actually, wait till you've read this bit, then close your eyes! Imagine the success already accomplished. As you visualise yourself, in your mind, having achieved the goal you set. How does it feel? Describe the emotions and write them down in the appropriate section of the 'TEARS of joy' worksheet. Are they strong emotions? Do they move you to want to act today? If they do, you are on track. If they don't, you may need to re-look at your goal, or think a bit deeper about what the achievement of that goal means in terms of you living a life of joyful longevity.

Thought – So here we are, right back at the very beginning again, and to the only one thing that really matters – your thoughts. Everything starts with a thought, a belief, or a perspective. It's your thoughts that will lead to the emotional state that will trigger the action that will start the process of developing the routine that will predictably result in any outcome you want in your life. So, that being the case, would you agree that the thoughts – the ones you choose to focus on – are the most important? Would it make sense to spend the time to really focus on your thoughts, wisely choose your thoughts, and explore your unconscious thoughts and how to change those not serving you?

You will need to go back to Chapters 6 and 7 and really dig deep into them. Read then re-read the content, own the concepts, and act on the strategies. Your life depends on your ability to become aware of your thoughts. Try to identify damaging thoughts, and make the necessary changes you need to make, no matter how challenging that may be. When you put down this book, again, it is your thoughts that will determine the outcomes in your life. Nothing else! When you own your thoughts, you will own your life.

Right now, as you look at the goal you have written in the *Success* section of the 'TEARS of joy' worksheet, what thought will set off the domino effect to bring you through to a joyful reality? The year eight student started with the thought that *he was dumb*, which led him to the results that reinforced that belief. After he and I worked through this worksheet together, just as you are doing now, his new thought about getting a B in Science was: '*I can and will do it. I can work and improve and achieve any result I want.*' Wow! Can you see the massive impact that one change of belief will make in his life? The difference in the next five, ten, twenty years and beyond will be mind-blowing. The *I am dumb* belief may well have led him to unemployment, drug use, crime, jail and, worst case, even death. Can you see where his new thought and belief will potentially lead him? These thoughts are worlds apart.

Write down your thought on the worksheet. Look at it, read it, affirm it, and repeat it many times each day. That thought, once an unconscious belief, will continue to bless your life for many years. This worksheet will change your life if you take it seriously. Complete it now, put it up somewhere obvious, read it every day and take the daily actions every day, for 63 days, and beyond.

63 days – Starting today

I'm nearly done. I can do no more for you. The rest is in your hands. What happens today and moving forward is up to you and is no one else's fault or responsibility. Are you okay with that? If so, and if it only takes 63 days to create strong, unbreakable neural pathways in the brain that will lead you to the 'TEARS of joy' you want, then would it be worth focusing for 63 days, starting today? If so, I want to offer you another resource that you will be able to download from my site at https:// andrewjobling.com.au/resources-downloads/.

AndrewJobling

ANDREWJOBLING.COM.AU

GOAL:

It is _____, and I feel _____

as I have _____.

I have rewarded myself with _____.

Why is the achievement of this goal important to you?

Creating Permanent Positive Change

Action 1 (A1)																					
Action 2 (A2)																					
Action 3 (A3)																					

First 21 days

Day	1	2	3	4	5	6	7	8	9	10	11	12	13	14	15	16	17	18	19	20	21
A1																					
A2																					
A3																					

Second 21 days

Day	1	2	3	4	5	6	7	8	9	10	11	12	13	14	15	16	17	18	19	20	21
A1																					
A2																					
A3																					

Third 21 days

Day	1	2	3	4	5	6	7	8	9	10	11	12	13	14	15	16	17	18	19	20	21
A1																					
A2																					
A3																					

Again, a very simple tool that seems like it's not a big deal, unless you use it and commit to it, then it's a life-changer. Refer to Chapter 13, where I discuss this tool in more detail and how to use it effectively. Can I make one suggestion right now? Start today!

Making the tears happen!

> Ephesians 2:10 – *For we are God's handiwork, created in Christ Jesus to do good works, which God prepared in advance for us to do.* (NIV)

I can't say much more than I have said already too many times in this book. I am guilty of repeating myself because I feel like the more I repeat it, the more you will get it. I apologise to the people who get it the first time, but that was never me. Maybe I'm writing this book for me, and you just get to read it. I just hope that, as you read the last section of this last chapter, the penny has dropped, the switch is flicked, the decision is made, and the moment for action is here.

My final plea is that you truly understand the greatest success, or a most dismal failure, starts with a single thought. That thought is one you can choose to either listen to and focus on, or question and disregard. It's a thought that you can change or let it rule your life. It's a thought that is your responsibility and no one else's.

I've been gobsmacked by the number of people convinced they are not in control of their thoughts. I have discussed this with several highly educated and informed people who, based on their upbringing, believe they are either lucky or unlucky and don't control their thoughts. I feel sorry for these people, because they will never experience the incredible 'TEARS of joy' that are available for them, and the same ones you are going to enjoy. You now know you are in control of your thinking because you can capture any emotion, identify the thoughts, and change them if you choose to.

<u>For the last time, some questions:</u>

What does success look like for you? Why is that important to you? What would be the consequences of not achieving it? Would that bother you? If so, why? What is one goal you need to achieve in the process of attaining that success? What habits need to be developed to make the goal a reality? What action will you start today to get the ball rolling? What emotional state will get you moving? In other words, how will it feel when you've achieved the goal? What thought will you focus on and affirm to spark that feeling?

I would like to pray for you if you are okay with that? As you read my prayer for you, I want to encourage you to really start to believe there is a source out there that can guide and direct you to the 'TEARS of joy' you want. I want to ask you to put logic aside and have faith that, when you start a course of action, the path forward to your joyful success will open for you. And one last thing, before I pray, and that is: why not open yourself to the possibility there is a God and having faith that God can help you in every area of your life? I started on my Christian path with that simple idea and hope, and I am glad that I did.

> *Heavenly Father, I thank you for placing this book in the hands of the person reading it right now. I thank you, God, as this person may not believe it was your work that moved them to read this book, they will take the messages in the book and apply them to their own lives. I pray you will give them the faith and courage to move forward in their life, knowing they are protected, guided, loved, and forgiven. Lord, I thank you for giving me the wisdom and*

courage to write this book. Thank you also for helping the reader believe in their own power and ability to focus on thoughts that will empower them. May the reader take the action needed and establish the habits to create wonderful abundance, and many 'TEARS of joy' moments in their life and the lives of others. You are a great God, and I have faith in your power in my life and the life of the person reading this prayer. Thank you, Father. Amen.

Your life is short. You only get one go at it. Make it your best. Fill it with 'TEARS of joy' experiences and live a truly wonderful life of joyful longevity. See how many lives you can influence and inspire as you go. Enjoy the journey that you have been put on this planet to experience. Go forth and let the 'TEARS of joy' flow!